The BLACK ART of HOLDEM

Appeasing the Poker Gods by:

Reading the ODDS
Building OPPORTUNITY
Creating YOUR LUCK

Ecallaw "Ratty" Leachim

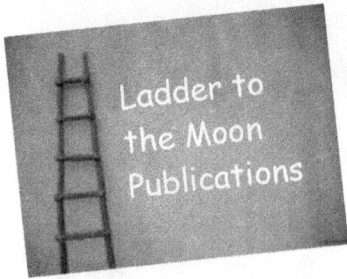

The **BLACK** ART of HOLDEM

Appeasing the Poker Gods by:
Reading the ODDS - Building OPPORTUNITY - Creating YOUR LUCK

This is not a book on how to PLAY poker. Everyone knows that, and there are hundreds of books out there on basic poker techniques. This book is all about how to make MONEY from poker. This is essentially knowing your opponents, understanding how to work them to create opportunity, and manufacture your LUCK.

The writer lost a fortune after the financial collapse of 2009 and has made a living out of playing poker since that time. Ecallaw has won major tournaments, State titles, National titles, but during the Covid19 crisis no poker games were being run. Just prior to this, at a friendly cash game, someone had suggested he write a book on the subject - So, with time rather than cards in his hands, he did!

As Ecallaw says, "There are just four modes people play in, and Seven Types of poker player. Picking what mix is present in the people at your table pretty much gives you the ability to KNOW the sort of cards they are holding. This gives you a tremendous advantage in betting and winning."

Discover how to shift the chips at any table towards your stack in simple, easy strategies that are proven to work.

May FORTUNA, the Goddess of Luck, be by your side

Vintage playing card -
The Queen of Hearts

The BLACK ART of HOLDEM

COPYRIGHT 2020 - Ladder to the Moon Publications
This book is published under the Berne Convention. All copyright
protected to the author. No prior use without permission except for
excerpts for review or educational purposes.
All enquiries via Email to: qrcaustralia@gmail.com
Published by Ladder to the Moon Publications.
ISBN: 978-0-6484277-4-2

https://www.law.cornell.edu/treaties/berne/overview.html

INDEX

In 1967 the fledgling game of Holdem was first played at the Golden Nugget in Las Vegas.

Inside four years, the WSOP would start and be moved to Binions Horseshoe where the infamy of Texas Holdem would go on to conquer the world!

Dedicated to Doyle Brunson
and the Holdem Pioneers

The Black Art of Holdem is a summary of all the principles of playing and winning Texas Holdem Poker. It is a complete and very easy to read reference packed into 142 pages. It includes:

- How to Spot the Type of Players on your Table
- Strategies on how to Maximize your Return in a Hand
- How to Work out your Odds in Seconds
- Understanding the Pot Value versus the Equity in your Hand
- Demonstrating ways to Create Opportunity and Make Luck
- How to play POSITION to Maximum Effect

The writer has won high stakes tournaments, State and National Titles, and has made a living from Poker for over a decade. This book will show you simple techniques and methods that will put you in control of any table.

When you control the action, you control the betting and you control the chips. This book shows you how to build massive chip stacks, win large cash prizes and have fun while doing it.

WELCOME

A t the time of writing this book, the Covid19 Pandemic is upon us. This means I can't make any money playing Poker, so I thought I might sit down to do what you are not supposed to do: reveal the secrets of how to consistently win playing Texas Holdem.

Without putting too fine a point on it, there is a whisper in your ear when you are holding gold, but do you hear it? And if you do, what do you DO about it?

I have always loved cards games. Hell, at age FOUR I was beating the adults in Canasta as a Trap Player! My Dad started his fortune on a game of Poker - he won a BSA 500 with sidecar and used that as a tool to get his beans to market. This got him out of the public service and eventually made him a rich man, Yes, he spent it all, but that is another story.

To introduce myself, they call me Ratty. Nice to meet you, and thank you for taking the time to look through this little collection of thoughts. First up: Everything you read is based on hard won experience. Here, you will find useful hints and tips and possibly an entirely new way of looking at the game of Texas Holdem.

As a player, I have won many State and National titles. In the course of time I have come against just about every type and size of competitor you could imagine. What I came to understand is that there are only seven basic types of Poker player, and four different ways that they play. I have made a lot of impossible calls and collected a lot of cash purely because I read the person correctly.

I trust you will find the **BLACK** Art of Holdem interesting - The goal was to give both the novice and the experienced player things to consider and ways to improve their play in this wonderful game. Your winnings will tell me if I succeeded.

The Worship of Luck and Opportunity

There is ample evidence that people still worship the ancient Sabine Gods of Luck (Fortuna) and Opportunity (Ops). You see the faithful praying to the Poker Gods at every Poker Tournament and Cash Game. All around the world, praying for luck in poker has become an obsession for millions of people. Precious few win much money, but in a curious sort of reverse positive, people DO come to know themselves better - Yes, this is usually when they are hanging down their heads, staring at their negatives while cursing themselves, going, "Mea Culpa" over their bad read while walking home, defeated. But self-awareness is self-awareness, how it arrives is merely the tool of instruction, or destruction as the case may be.

Poker is an extremely popular sport. Some would say it is almost a religion across the world right now. It is possibly the worlds most played game, both as an online presence and in "real life". Yet Poker is a game that opposes what most people would consider as "sporting" because in THIS game you are respected by how well you lie, cheat and deceive. The entire game is based on THREE OPTIONS - Call, Raise or Fold. Do this right and you win other people chips. Whether you steal, bluff or win them doesn't matter - what matters is learning to do this consistently. To get chips you need to understand people and how strong they are in any given hand. This is called "Getting a Read" and if you do this well you will Fold, Call or Raise at the right times. This will equal cash in your pocket and put a smile on your face.

FORTUNA
Goddess of Luck

You might note by the image that Goddess Fortuna looks a whole lot like what the Catholic church painted as a guardian angel. It is no coincidence that angels, invented in the 5th century, were modelled after her. In this book we will discuss strategies and ways to encourage your 'guardian angel' to come and sit beside you at the Poker table.

Fools stand on their island of opportunities and look toward another land. There is no other land; there is no other life but this.
Thoreau

What is this Thing Called Texas Hold-Em?

There are hundreds of books on Poker of how to play better, win more and understand the psychology of the game. So - the first question! Why is this book any better than the rest? You will have to decide for yourself - This book is SPECIFICALLY for Texas Hold-em. It is not theory nor is it specialized knowledge - it is all common sense, based on thousands and thousands of games and millions of hands.

EVERYTHING in poker is based around reading the table and playing your position. Understanding your opponents and getting a handle about how they see you is the start point. From here, you spot your opportunity and create luck. Secondary to this, but essential, are the cards you are dealt. We all imagine getting pocket Aces (A A) is the dream, but play them wrong and they become a nightmare. (So many people leave tournaments head down, losing with AA.)

WHAT you see, HOW you act, and WHEN you fold make the difference between winning and losing. So how do we play our cards right? Or in other words, how do we consistently win?

First up: How many players, when they are dealt cards, look at them right away? This is an easy question to answer: *every non-professional player in the world.* First Principle to consider: The LAST thing you should look at in any given hand are the cards you hold.

But WHY? Surely the cards are what is the most important thing? No, how you are seen and what you see is far more important than the cards you are dealt. You should first be looking for OPPORTUNITY, which in poker equates to weakness in other players.

The Robbie Burns poem "To a Louse" should be tattooed on the heart of every poker player:

O wad some Power the giftie gie us
To see oursels as ithers see us!
It wad frae mony a blunder free us,
An' foolish notion:
What airs in dress an' gait wad lea'e us,
An' ev'n devotion!

Translation: *"Oh what power the Giver (Gods) gives us, to see ourselves as others see us. It would from many a blunder free us, and foolish notion. What airs in dress and gait would leave us, and even devotion!"*

This is, in a nutshell, the game we call Poker. Seeing others as they are, then going further and perceiving how YOU are seen. From this point of understanding we THEN play the cards we have been dealt.

Poker is a brutally honest game that is, paradoxically, based on deception and lies. It rips our airs and graces from us, tramples on our ideals and makes us look ridiculous - yet we poor foolish poker players just keep coming back for more! Why?

I suspect it is because we find some sort of dark grace in the shadows of our psyche, where in both our crushing defeats and glorious victories, Poker reveals us to ourselves, as we are.

It is a war with the mind - no more and no less than an all-out conflict disguised as a social pleasantry. Of all the games we play, there are few more brutal than Texas Holdem in its psychic brittleness.

"The history of poker is a matter of some debate. The name of the game likely descended from the French poque, which descended from the German pochen ('to knock'), but it is not clear whether the origins of poker itself lie with the games bearing those names. It closely resembles the Persian game of as nas, and may have been taught to French settlers in New Orleans by Persian sailors. It is commonly regarded as sharing ancestry with the Renaissance game of primero and the French brelan. The English game brag (earlier bragg) clearly descended from brelan and incorporated bluffing (though the concept was known in other games by that time). It is quite possible that all of these earlier games influenced the development of poker as it exists now."
(Doylebrunson.com)

A Zero Sum Game

Poker is like the Options Market - It is a game where nothing is created. A lot of money is made - but only at the expense of other investors in the hand. And, just like playing the Options Market, you win by how well you pick your OPTIONS in any given hand

Tournament Poker is a Zero-Sum Game. The money that goes INTO the pot, either in the hand or in the tournament, is what comes OUT. One person wins, or you might split - but essentially one wins while the others lose.

You always have THREE options at any given point - You fold your cards, (give up the hand) you call the ante, (what every hand costs you to play) or you raise. (make a bet) Obviously if someone raises before you act, you can re-raise the 'action' in a hand.

Your "read" is much like an investor predicting if something will run well or fail. This determines your action. The accuracy of your read decides whether you win or lose. Yet there is a science in the middle of the gamble. The game of Poker revolves around Opportunity and Luck - But winning CHIPS is based on picking your openings to play or fold and THIS is based around how well you understand your opponents.

All over the world, at this very minute there are people making a lot of money in poker games - which only means there are ALSO a lot of people losing money. It is a ZERO SUM GAME.

Now, if I ask which side of the coin you want to be on, we all know you would see yourself as a winner. But sadly, most of us let our negatives take charge. THIS is what creates the losers at any table. The majority of players get lost in their own narrative and forget to read the others in their hand. Thus, they miss the subtle signals, the opportunities to either call, fold or raise.

Bad Beats aside, *most people defeat themselves in Poker.*

Poker is a Game of Observation

Poker is a game of awareness disguised as Cards. The accuracy of your PERCEPTION determines outcomes. Do you see your opponents as strong or weak? This will determine your actions, and your actions determine you outcomes. And remember: You are ALSO being seen. You are also being judged. We all get the odd losing streak and show frustration - Others will sense this and bid you out of pots. Show weakness and you soon discover there is ALWAYS someone to capitalize on your faults. Discipline your moods, focus your mind, and LISTEN.

Oh what gift the Givee give us, etc.

If you are not consistently winning, if you are not consistently on final tables, YOU are the one at fault. Yes, we all get Bad Beats where you call someone's 'All-In' with your pocket pair - they then flip over 2/ 5 and jag two pair on the flop. You cannot avoid luck, but if you understand the table, see the players clearly, you CAN predict how they will act. If you can see something clearly you CAN negotiate it.

This book will turn you into the person who consistently WINS.

So, how do you win on a regular basis? Obviously, you have to understand the math - but after that It is all about the READ! It all starts with a good read - not this book - a good read on the people at your table. The GOOD news - It's not so hard to pick the type of person you are playing against. There are only seven basic types of poker player and Four Modes they play with - we will discuss them here.

The BAD news - YOU are ALSO a type and someone can as easily get a read on YOU. The message is simple: Get a read not just on the players at your table but also on how 'you' are seen, then work with this. This will gain you more chips than luck ever did.

O wad some Power the giftie gie us

To see oursels as ithers see us!

If you can remember this, engrave it into your brain, you will become a winner. How you are seen is EVERYTHING, how you see others is EVERYTHING. Cards are secondary. If you are to win consistently, you MUST watch and observe what the table is doing, who you are playing, what signals they are sending, as well as what you might be advertising.

By learning to play more methodically and with greater focus, you will develop what is called a "Table Presence" - where you learn to set up the image of the "type" of player you are.

After this you learn to convincingly lie about all of the above, this is the Black Art and where you start to play this game called Holdem.

Classic Case Scenario: *You peel up Aces - the strongest pre-flop hand in Hold-Em. How do you react? How do you bet to capitalize on the cards? You know you are ahead of everyone, but you ALSO know that AA and KK are the hands you most often exit a tournament with.*

If you know the types of players at your table, have developed a table presence, and have a sense of where the LUCK is running for other player - only then can you bet in the correct way to maximize your gain, or minimize your loss.

General Introduction

"I don't gamble, if you will concede that poker is a game of skill."
— *Robert A. Heinlein*

Most people reading this will already be familiar with Poker and in particular, the variation known as Texas Holdem. The game, as the name implies, comes from Robsville, Texas. Introduced to Las Vegas in 1963 by Corky McCorquodale it attracted interest from leading gamblers. its popularity comes from Crandell Addington, Doyle Brunson, and Amarillo Slim playing a version where Aces were seen as both the lowest and the highest card in the deck. It is this specific variation that we are dealing with in this tome.

In Texas Holdem, each player at a table receives TWO CARDS, face down. These are known as Hole Cards. There are two 'forced' hands called the Small and Big Blind. If the "blinds", as these forced bets are known, are two dollars, the Big must put in two dollars while the Small must put in one dollar. The Blinds sit to the LEFT of the dealer button.

Doyle Brunson 1976 WSOP Tournament

The game he famously won playing with a Ten and a Two

The dealer button denotes who is the dealer in that hand, and it moves around one step to the LEFT every hand. Which is to say, after every hand is finished, the Small Blind takes up the dealer position.

The Big Blind represent the MINIMUM bet. In tournament play, the Blind goes up in set increments throughout the tournament. They are in place to force action, particularly late in the tournament. This is very important, for it denotes the MAIN difference between a cash game with set blinds and the tournament.

You need a lot of chips to wage war towards the end of a tournament. When it comes to 500 table tournaments, you need a lot of chips to even pay a blind by the end of the day. *Tournament chips are LIMITED.* They represent a Zero Sum Game where the chips in the tournament are the total chips possible. No more come in or go out.

Therefore, they are worth more than chips in a cash game, where you can endlessly re-buy. This is the essential difference between the two forms of Poker and it forms a VAST difference in large tournaments.

Cash games are a sprint, tournaments are a marathon. Cash games are all about buying hands and bluffing whereas tournaments are more about survival. Winners in either game are those who find the correct balance between these two poles.

After you receive your first two cards, betting starts from "Under the Gun" - which is the position to the immediate left of the Big Blind. To stay in the hand you must pay the minimum of the Blind, which represents a "Call", or you can choose to "Raise" which must be any figure that is double the Blind, or higher. If you do not like your cards, you can "Fold" by presenting the cards (face down) to the dealer.

Texas Holden is generally played as "Unlimited" which means you can raise ANY amount as long as it is above the minimum raise. This is to say, at any time you can put ALL your chips in as a bet, called an "All In".

Betting is the crux of the game - Each Hand has FOUR LAYERS of betting: Pre-flop, the Flop, The Turn and the River. These betting layers are called "Streets" and represent an opportunity to bet or fold. In a Holdem game your position on the table represents your position in the "Action" - which is to say when you can act.

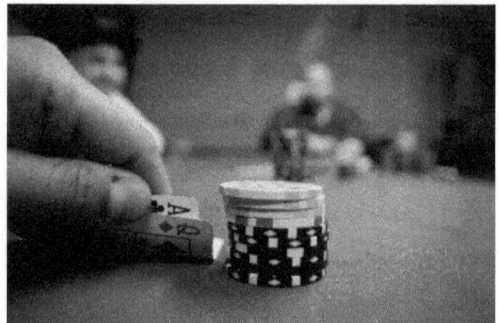

Pre-flop, first to act is Under the Gun, post-Flop, first to act is the Small Blind. You have a round of betting pre-Flop, another round ON the Flop, a third round on the Turn card, with a final round of betting on the River.

When it comes to the last person to act on the River, this is the end of betting - or in situations when ALL players in the hand are "All In". All cards are then exposed and the dealer will determine the winner.

However, the winner may have been "All In" with a small chip stack. You can only win the amount of the bet from each player that you have bid. If there are chips left in the "Pot" (the collected aggregate of chips that have been bet) then the person who came Second will pick up the remainder of the chips. (obviously, you cannot win more chips from any one player that is more that the amount of chips you have bet with)

The point is that this is a BETTING game. You seek to control the "Action" with betting, but at any given time, any person in any hand can "Push" - which is to say they can bet all their chips. If they are called, it is then a race to the River to see who wins.

Winning a pot is great, but the SIZE of the pot is far more important than the number of pots won. So the crucial part to playing Texas Holdem is BETTING in such a way so as to maximize your return.

In this book we will be looking at how to alter the odds in our favor by understanding the type of people who are playing at your table. From this understanding, we will learn how to create openings, or opportunity, with each type you will meet. Done well, it appears to people watching that you are a 'lucky' player.

It is not 'luck' but the ability to read and feed your Odds by understanding WHO and WHAT is at your table. From here you create your Opportunities, and appear to generate Luck.

As they say in the movie, "Rounders" - It is NOT luck that lands the same players again and again at the final table of major tournaments. This book will give you insights on how to become a player who consistently lands on the Final Table.

Ops - Goddess of Fertility - The word Opportunity comes from from her.

Basics of Texas Holdem Poker

The game is very straightforward. Before dealing, two people put money into the Pot, the Small Blind, and the Big Blind. They sit to the LEFT of the Dealer Button. The Dealer Button migrates to the LEFT after every hand is finished.

There is a set price to play a hand, called the BLIND. In CASH games this is a specific amount that does not change. In TOURNAMENTS, the price goes up at set intervals through the game. If the BLIND is set at 100, this is the MINIMUM BET you can make. When the Blinds raise to 200, this then becomes the minimum bet.

You are dealt TWO CARDS. These are called your HOLE CARDS. There is a round of BETTING after these are dealt, starting with "Under the Gun" who is the player to the left of the Big Blind. Players will CALL the minimum bet, they will FOLD, or they will RAISE. To stay in the hand you must equal any call or raise that is made.

When the first round of betting is done, one card is BURNED (placed face down) from the top of the deck, and three cards are dealt, face up. These are COMMUNITY CARDS. These first three cards are called the FLOP. There is another round of betting on the FLOP by whoever is left in the hand. Only ACTIVE players keep their cards.

When done, another BURN card is placed face down, and a SINGLE card is placed face up. This is the TURN. Another round of betting ensues, and when done, the LAST CARD is dealt.

Again, one card is BURNED, face down. Another is dealt face up, called the RIVER. A final round of betting ensues, the best five cards, based on the combination of your HOLE cards and the COMMUNITY cards determines the winner.

Texas Holdem retains all the standard hand rankings of conventional (stud) poker, but with two Hole Cards and Five Community Cards, the chances for straights and flushes are higher than in five card stud.

An example hand on the following page gives a brief rundown on how much an individual hand changes as the Flop runs to the Turn, then to the River.

EXAMPLE

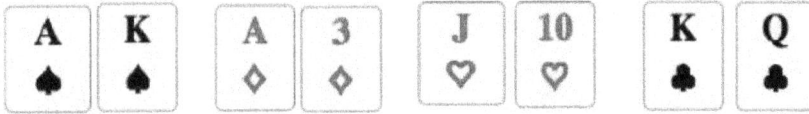

| Sue | Mark | Bob | Sally |

FLOP

On the FLOP Sally is well ahead with TWO PAIR. Two KINGS and Two QUEENS

TURN

On the TURN Mark is well ahead with an ACE HIGH STRAIGHT

Yet the RIVER makes the ULTIMATE HAND for BOB - The ROYAL FLUSH.

RIVER

The MADNESS of Holdem is shown here. On EVERY STREET (The Flop, Turn and River are called Streets) a different person was winning.
- *Pre-Flop SUE was in front with A K suited.*
- *SUE then thought she was good with the paired King on the FLOP.*
- *But SALLY was in the lead with TWO PAIR.*
- *Yet, BOB had hit and has a FLUSH DRAW.*
- *The TURN puts MARK to the top of the pile with a STRAIGHT.*
- *Yet BOB has hit TWO PAIR and can get a FULL HOUSE or a FLUSH*
- *Finally, the RIVER gives BOB the WIN with a Royal Flush.*

Texas Holdem is a Betting Game

"The secret to success is to start from scratch and keep scratching ~
Doyle Brunson

O nce you understand the patterns that underlie how people play, you will find most of the people at your table are predictable. So how do you discover this? You work out how people play through betting and seeing how they react. *Betting is the language of Poker.*

In Texas Holdem, the goal is to maximize return and minimize risk. In every hand these MUST be considerations. In simple terms, you are there to get chips - In lieu of this, there are two principles to remember.

First Principle: Unless you have the absolute NUTZ (the best hand possible) you DO NOT want to see the River. You want people to FOLD before the River card is turned. Sixty Two percent of all hands are won on the River, if it is seen. This means that if you are ahead on the Turn, you have a sixty two percent chance of being behind on the River card.

Second Principle: If you DO have the NUTZ you have to fish for chips. You are literally trying to catch a fat one. We will look at how best to do this through HOW you bet, raise, or fold.

At all times: If your hand CAN be beaten, apply the First Principle. There is NO advice I can give you that is more powerful than this - act in such a way that people WANT TO FOLD before the River is seen.

Betting is a LANGUAGE. A large pre-flop raise means you are saying clearly you have a big hand, or you are lying. EITHER is part of the language of betting. A large raise on the flop might be saying you have hit well, or that you have a massive draw, or nothing at all.

When you BET, you are BIDDING in the same way as someone bids at an auction. You are asking a QUESTION, which might be, "How good are your cards?" Good players massage the table by ASKING, via betting, if anyone is interested in arguing the hand.

Pushing 'All In' is a STATEMENT, saying,"I have this." When you go "All In" on the River, you are STATING several possibilities: You could be bluffing, you could hold the world - the point is, if you are not ASKING question, you putting people up against a wall and holding a gun to their head. This is also a valid poker strategy. The point is, you bet to encourage people to think about where they are at

By asking questions before you make a statement, by watching the reaction of players in the hand, you can get a feel of your position in the hand. Betting correctly is asking a question and looking for a response. It is how you win in Hold-em - It is the black art of the entire game.

Painting the Picture

The psychology of betting is all about painting a picture, drawing images in the opponents imagination. *This is what generates your Opportunity.* Keep in mind that NOT BETTING can do this as effectively as betting. You might flop a monster, as they say - a hand that would be very difficult to beat. You may choose NOT to bet and allow others to catch up. Why? To create an Opportunity! When you have the best hand, you really want others to believe you are weak and bet INTO you.

It is all about the betting. You hear about how people "create luck" - This is true, but it is done through BETTING. You BET in such a way that you create the impression you have the winning hand and, unless you are walking into the nuts, (The best possible hand) you create doubt in the other players minds. Doubt opens the door to fear, fear creates a sense of failure and this means opponents will often fold better hands.

People mostly call your raise on the basis of what is known as their "Outs". These are the cards they believe they are calling for which will give them the pot. If you paint the picture well, unless they get the card they are seeking, they will fold. Apply Principle One - Liberally - *You do not want them to see the river*, so bet accordingly.

What's an Out?

An "Out" is a card you need to win. It is a value is based on percentages - if a person has eight "Outs" (at roughly two percent per "Out") they have a calling equity of 16%. Two cards to come = 32% of what is called Equity in the Pot. If someone has a 32% equity, most players will call any raise that is less than 32% of the net Pot.

Rule of Thumb: *If your bet means a players call will be 30% of what is to be won, most players with eight or more "Outs" will call you.*

BETTING EQUITY EXAMPLE

They Hold

You Hold

The Pot is 10K. You land TWO PAIR. You bet 1/3rd the pot - 3500. J K Clubs CALLS - they have VALUE to CALL. The TURN gives a nothing. You now have to bet ENOUGH to get him off the Pot. The bet must not give him VALUE to call. Against 17K in the pot he now has an 18% equity to call, or 3000 - You must bet MORE THAN 3K. Most will bet 6K to get him to fold.

They Hold

They Hold

You Hold

This is a VERY DIFFERENT scenario. The person to your right has landed a STRAIGHT. You don't know it, but now YOU are the one chasing. You have bet 6K on the TURN, making a 23K pot. J 9 is not stupid - they KNOW they are ahead, yet the River can kill them - They go ALL IN!

What do you do? You listen to the language of the betting, just as J K should fold to your 6K Bet on the TURN, you should fold to the Re-Raise to your 6K. The reasons for this are many, the potential straight on the FLOP is obvious, but the four on the TURN will have given 5 6 a straight. Your two pair may be facing trips, or a better two pair. You should fold.

USE BETTING as a LANGUAGE

We design our betting to get feedback on what a person might have and to see where we stand. Once we have a good idea what we are against, THEN we bet sufficient to drive them to fold, or maybe THEY push and WE are the ones having to chose, call or fold.

Sounds simple enough, know your math, be smart, you will win. If only this were true! The catch is this - no one betting strategy works on all players. Almost NO hands are unbeatable before the River. You have to know the right gambit to play at the right moment, based on who is at the table and what you read as the strength of their hands.

I cannot tell you the number of players I have met who will push ALL IN with the Flush Draw on the flop. Bad play on one hand, but better to be driving the bus than be a passenger. If you are going over the cliff at least you will see where you are going to land!

To use betting as a language successfully you have to understand the TYPES of people you are playing. Why? Because each type has a different set of behaviors. The loose-aggressive pushes with their flush draw where the tight aggressive does not. If you pick them as tight-aggressive (TAG) they are telling YOU they have the straight. But a TAG will generally have waited until YOU bet before pushing.

Every hand comes with a set of decisions. We target our betting to match the 'type' we find in front of us and then we bet to get them to call or fold. That is pretty much IT - the game of poker in a nutshell.

That said, there are many fine points and subtle tricks to the game of Texas Holdem. It is a brazenly simple game, one that a four year-old can grasp, yet one where an Eighty year-old can still be learning to play properly. What we are here to learn is not just how to WIN, and fool can win a hand in Holdem. More importantly, we need to learn how to maximize our return in any hand we play. The ONLY thing that matters in this game is the size of the pots you win.

Anyone can win a pot, precious few can milk the return for all it is worth. The black art to gaining a maximum return comes from an understanding of the types of players we are likely to meet. When you KNOW who you have in front of you learn how to get chips from them.

These next pages help you identify the style and type of Poker Player you will meet on every table. First up are the FOUR MODES.

The FOUR MODES

On every table you will meet four basic "modes" or overall strategies on how people play the game. This is the first and relatively easy "tell" you are given when you sit at any table.
The Four Basic Modes are:
- Passive: Sits and waits for cards, rarely bets out
- Aggressive: Bets often and hard.
- Loose: Calls or bets with any two cards. Plays for luck.
- Tight: Plays only High Card, Suited Connected or Pockets.

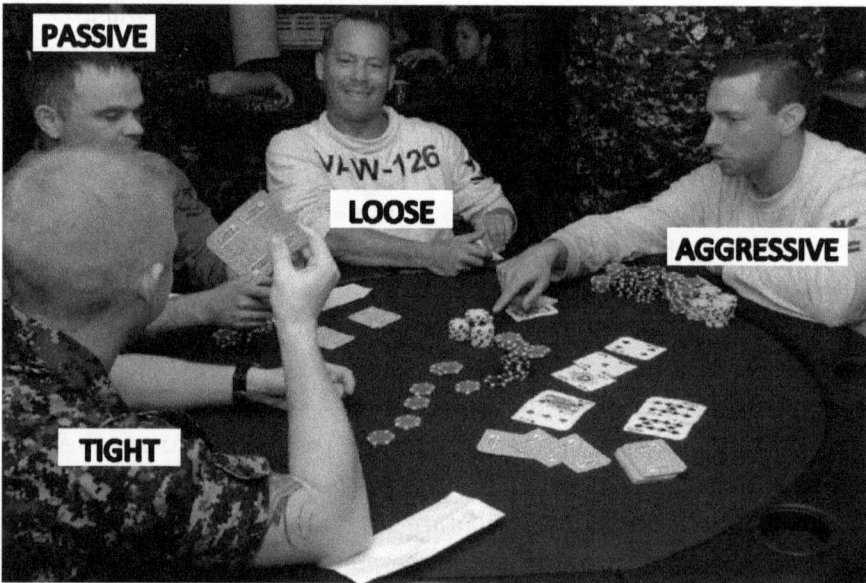

There is no 'pure' style - every player is a mix of the above and some players work a different style every hand they play, but it is fair to say that Pot Buyers generally play aggressive and loose, while Trap Players work with Passive and Tight.

The style someone will play may depend on their reason for being at the table. There are a series of questions we must ask ourselves if we are to work out where the player is sitting with the above modes.

Are they recreational players? Are they here to socialize, have a drink, and meet people. It's a night out! This is a high percentage of the players you meet. These people tend to be a little loose because they are there have fun, and a gamble is fun.

Are they a regular at this venue? These are the ones that know everyone there and, as a result, they also know how they play. Regulars are there to cash, not to just have some fun. These people play a fairly predictable game.

Are they a Pro or Semi-Pro? You see them at the higher buy in games, and they are fairly easy to pick. They are attentive and quiet for the most part. A Pro player is there to make money, so they are rarely at low stakes games.

At Casinos you can also get "Prop Players" - These are people employed by the Casino who 'prop up' the game. No one wants to sit at an empty poker table, so they attract 'sitters' from the public. They play with their own money, but are paid a small salary to be there.

There are variations and combinations of all the above.

You can have a regular recreational player, as one example. But the recreational player doesn't really pay a lot of attention to how others play the game and are not focused on winning the overall game so much as the hand they are in. The Prop Player is often a regular and occasionally a professional who is happy to have they stake covered by management. You even find recreational professionals, usually old guys who really know the game who just like to fish the fishes at the odd casino for spare change.

Why is this important? When you accurately pick where the people in front of you are at before you seriously start to play any hands, you can then adjust your game to capitalize on them.

Aggression is only one tendency to look at when sizing up your opponents. How many hands they play, regardless of their behavior when playing them, is how you measure whether your opponent is loose or tight.

A loose poker player gets involved in a lot of pots. They play a large percentage of hands. A tight poker player doesn't play in a lot of pots. Tight players usually fold in the face of aggression.

Tight poker isn't always better than loose poker, but generally speaking, it's better to play your hands selectively.

When you combine aggression levels with looseness, you get four basic categories of player:

Maniacs: Reckless folk who play anything and bet large.

Rocks: As the name implies, steadfast and solid.

Calling Stations: Call with anything, chase for anything.

TAGs: Tight Aggressive Players - these are the ones who make money.

Betting Variations

There are a range of betting styles a player may choose. As one simple example, there is the CHECK RAISE. You check the Flop, and when someone raise the Pot, you RE-RAISE their raise.

This is traditionally done when you flop a huge hand and WANT someone to bet in. Or, you want it to LOOK like this with a bluff, or, you are really testing how well the raiser has hit. All are perfectly valid. You would be surprised how often a player does a raise in the dealer position to a checked flop and the re-raise causes him to fold.

There is a similar strategy when you have an aggressive player, which is to double their raise, regardless of your position on the table. If you want to STAY IN THE HAND, a simple doubling of the raise is often enough to get the player to check it to the river.

In NO LIMIT Holdem, the only limit is the size of your chip stack. You have to bet the MINIMUM, which is whatever the blinds are at that point, but you can bet anything above that. In most games, there is a protocol of betting "In Turn", which is to say, from the first to act in any given hand, the NEXT to act is the next live hand to their left.

Basic guidelines are: A standard three times the blind pre-Flop is telling the table you have a big hand. A POT Sized bet on the Flop is telling the table "I got this." Let's say you are in a hand with a good player, they go three times the blind pre-Flop. The Flop runs Q 7 5, and they bet the pot - They probably have A Q. When they make the same Raise POST Flop as they did pre-Flop, they probably have A K of middle pockets. This is NOT a given, but it's a basic outline.

When someone raises three or four times the blind and a solid player pushes back with All In on that raise, they are telling you they have Aces or Kings, or they are bluffing. This is the LANGUAGE of Poker speaking, or at least, it is supposed to be.

In truth, in most games people are not consistent and bet without rhyme or rhythm. I will say this, if you DO bet consistently and strongly, the better players will note it, and this WILL affect whether they call or fold any given hand.

Seven Types of Poker Player

"When a man with money meets a man with experience, the man with experience leaves with money and the man with money leaves with experience." **Anonymous**

The Faithful Dogs of Poker

There is a very good reason dogs don't play poker - They would wag their tails with any good hand! Picking your players, getting a read, and understanding the type of play you can expect from a person means you are forewarned and ready to deal with anything.

You have come to a table of strangers. In a few hands you have started to pick the MODE, whether they are loose or tight, etc. Now we want to focus on who we have in front of us.

As soon as we sit we must start the process of recognising the TYPE of poker player we have. This is the easy part - there are only seven basic types. Yet, this is like the seven notes you find in any key of music - no song is made of a single note - There are many and various mixes of the archetypes at any given table and everyone there will sing their own variation to these themes. The HARD part is working out what song they are singing in the hand you are in. Remember, no two poker players are the same, yet they ALL play within a TYPE as listed below.

Keep in mind these are STEREOTYPES and that every player has a little bit of each within their Soul. How much of each is the perennial question. Plus professional players will often mimic these stereotypes. EG: A person may appear like a drunk donkey, yet they are anything but. People will play the fool to get you off your game.

Donkey: (Fish) This is a person who makes large irrational bets, or calls, regardless of position or cards. This type have many sub-sets, but the most common is termed the Donkey. (A person who calls raises with nothing and wins the pot with unlikely cards) The Calling Station, the person who calls every pre-flop bet, is another variation. But the pure blood enemy of all good poker is the Cherry Bomber. They don't just call your Raise, they BOMB - they push regardless of the cards they hold.

Pot Buyer: This type of player regularly seeks to bet in position, with or without cards, in order to control the table.

The Big Man: *The Rock, the Chinese, the Texan.* The ones who stay in and keeps calling because they have hit something or hold an Ace. They fear loss of face, etc. (It is NOT always a man, obviously)

The Old Woman: Safety Player. Raises only with AA or KK, and sometimes not even then. (It is NOT always a woman, obviously)

The Chaser: People who chase for cards. (Main variations below)

A/ Pre-flop: Calls any raise that is less than three times the blind. Wants to see what hits.

B/ On the Flop: Calls any draw. Calls or Re-Raises any flush draw/open ender or situation with Eight or more outs.

C/ On the Turn or River: Calls any three times the blind raise with any pair, regardless of the board

D/ Variation called The Doubter: One who calls any three times the blind raise to the River because they have an Ace or pocket pair, regardless of the board.

Trap Player: The most dangerous. These people DO NOT raise with good cards. They wait for a raise hoping to catch the pot buyer, cherry bomber, etc.

The Professional: Far more common now-a-days. Pro and semi-pro players are rarely seen at low stakes tournaments, however.

A/ by the book: The player raises with two high cards, re-raises the flop, checks to river when called.

B/ Bet to Discover: This type of Player raises to get a read.

C/ Small Baller: Drives out weaker players with constant nibble bets

D/ Position Player: Always calls (and often raises) when they are on or before the dealer button. If the flop is checked to them, they will look to steal the pot.

How to Pick What You Got

All players are a mix of these seven essential ingredients. The trick is picking what is the dominant stereotype that is running the person you are dealing with. Keep in mind, people act differently with different people at different times, so you can only do this for the hand you are presently in. Suffice to say, however, if the person is in every pot, calling whatever is raised, it's a fair bet to say they are a Donkey, Maniac or Loose Aggressive player.

So, you have a rough idea of what you have at the table - The next trick is knowing when to be a hand with any of the above. EG: If you have Kings or Aces, you will call ALL of them, but suited connected against a Trap Player you would be more careful with, while snapping a call with these to a raise by a Pot Buyer.

It is almost impossible to cover all the variations, but let me try with an example to give you a basic guideline.

Pre-Flop

You Have 7H / 8H (Suited Connected Hearts) In the hand there is a person you read as Trap Player. There is an Old Woman, and a Pot Buyer. You are last to act. Pot Buyer is first, and he raises. Trap Player just calls, Old Woman Calls. You are reasonably confident you are against at least four cards over your 7 / 8 so you are playing for the flush or straight - You are at 22% equity with suited connected.

Do you Raise, Call or Fold? A Raise will most likely get the Old Woman out, but if she has pockets, AK or AQ she will stay. Trap Player will just call, unless he has high pockets, then he will push. Pot Buyer will call any double or triple his initial raise pre-flop.

You RAISE. You need more information and you want to tell the other players you have a hand. And you MIGHT! What you are really doing is forcing people to CHOOSE. Let's say they all just call - and you have Old Woman on AK, Trap Player on middle pockets or AK / AQ, with the Pot Buyer on just about anything. Let's look at what is really happening.

| Pot Buyer | Trap | Old Woman | You Hold |

 The Flop - It has something for everyone

Now it gets interesting. Pot Buyer, as first to act, WILL raise. He will test if anyone has anything. Trap player will call, he wants more chips in the Pot - It will be the Old Woman who will push here. She WILL go ALL IN because this is exactly the flop she thought she was looking for. The question is, what do I do?

Here is the quandary - I pretty much know the Old Woman player has high pockets now. I am ahead, yet I know the Pot Buyer has something. The Trap player looks happy - I am putting him on a straight or trips. I WANT to call, but I know I need a 7 or 8. Four cards left in the deck - 8% per card. Do I bet my game on getting an 8% draw on the next card?

I fold, knowing that someone will call and I will see if it was a good or bad choice. I am grateful I am last to act because I might have pushed if I was first. The Pot Buyer and the Trap player both call. We know the Turn - it is a 4 Diamonds. All players are 'All In' - cards are now exposed.

| 8 ♣ | 7 ♣ | 10 ♠ | 4 ♦ | 2 ♥ | J ♠ | 9 ♦ | Trap WINS |

The Old Woman cannot win by the Turn. She needed to push pre-Flop, which would have gotten the Trap Player out, and myself. The Pot Buy needs a CLUB. The River comes - it is a blank - the Straight holds up.

Now, why is this important? If I had been in the hand with a Pot Buyer, Old Woman and a Donkey - I would have called the 'All In'. But because I picked the Trap Player I folded and lived to play another hand.

The DETACHED Player

When you are playing poker well, you learn to use all of the above stereotypes and all the different modes at random in your game. In this way, you become the EIGHTH PLAYER. This is a knowing mix of any or all of the previous types where you, as the player, select the type of person you need to be in any given hand.

This makes you a more random competitor, thus far more difficult to read. This is the Holy Grail, to become the unreadable player. Why? Every decent poker player makes their decisions based on what they read in your actions. When you are truly detached you find you are not so transparent, but as important as being unreadable is, being able to read others and react accordingly is THE game winning strategy. You are more able to see clearly what is in front of you. You are better able to mimic each of the types your opponents know and recognize.

In this way they cannot get a handle on what you are, who you are, or what you hold. You become the detached observer.

The Detached Observer doesn't care about the cards, just position, pot value, and who they pick as weak playing in the hand. They then choose any one of the aforementioned types to act out according to their read of the table and will do so apparently at random - but it is really a calculated guess, based on observation and guesstimation. Suffice to say - Luck is the only thing that beats them.

The really crazy thing, a Pot Buyer will think you are just Pot Buying when you raise. A Trap Player will see a Trap when you just call or check. The Professional will see another Professional because they see you as Tight / Aggressive, while the Donkey will see another chance to donkey someone. Only the Big Man, Old Woman or Chaser will see nothing, because they are too fixated on their own cards.

What Type is This?

You are about to go to a table, and a guy looking like this turns up. What do you make of him? He looks like a mix between a pot buyer and a donkey, but when you see him in action, he plays tight, despite the fact he talks loud.

A lot more players are turning up in disguise! They dress and act one way, to convince you they are a larrikin or a fool. Do not judge the book by the cover - judge by HOW THEY PLAY. This is the only way you can truly measure a person.

Rule of Thumb: If someone is intentionally drawing attention to themselves, they are generally trying to get you look away from what they are doing.

SUMMARY:

In the next chapter we will go over in detail these various 'types' but know in advance, no person is purely ONE type of Poker Player. Like the ingredients in the Macarthur's Park cake, all your brilliant observations can be left out in the rain and washed away by your inattention to the prevailing weather conditions.

For Example: The person you picked as a Donkey was really a professional Trap Player, waiting for you to walk in to his parlour. There were clues, but you got over confident in your read. NOTHING IS FIXED!

Please try to remember, there is nothing in Poker but the next card, the present moment, and the chips you hold. How you play the present is what will create the future, yet it won't change the next card.

Poker is a balance between confidence, ability and common sense - but the best and most carefully thought out plan can be shattered when next card that falls. The best players smile with the bad beats and keep punching away. Observation of the types of players at your table increases your percentages, but doesn't remove risk!

However, we CAN lessen our risk by guessing at HOW the various types of player at your table will react. We get into a study of them on the following pages, as well as gambits to negotiate their methods.

However, right up front, let me point out that when dealing with what we call the Cherry Bomber, there IS no strategy. I will be dealing with them first, because they have become a plague in both on-line and real life poker games. I will not be dealing with any other game bar Texas Holdem, but for most forms of Poker what I say will hold true. In Pot Limited Games, such as Omaha, Cherry Bombers are constrained. (but playing Omaha is another book entirely)

Remember, every hand and every player is different. Any person who suggests a set way to play your cards is a fool. What we will be talking about are ways to act which sets up a rhythm, a mood that which creates a 'sense of fate' in the minds of other players.

When you know and understand the types you are dealing with on a table you can refine the strategies I will outline. Do it right and, in time, you will become an almost unbeatable player.

Remember: A person just one inch ahead wins the race - and no one celebrates coming second. Every inch of advantage improves your odds of winning. And knowing your Poker types is a MAJOR inch forward.

The Donkey

A "Donkey" is essentially a person who plays for luck. They do not know their odds, their pot values or anything at all - If they like their cards they call any raise. Originally, this type was called a "Fish" - a person who loved to fish for cards. The typical Donkey is the person who has an Ace or small pockets who calls any raise pre-flop and any raise to the River. They will even call a River raise without hitting anything, but if they hit a card, especially an Ace, they will call ANY raise.

Most believe this type is the bane of all professional players. This is incorrect, real players LOVE having a donkey or two at their table. However, the variation of the Donkey known as the Cherry Bomber is a problem. We will come to this shortly - First we must define the "type" so we are all on the same page.

The Donkey Player is insensitive to the language of betting, they have no awareness of odds and they have little concept of pot value and what hands they should be in, or otherwise. They are more "Pokies" (poker machine) players than Poker Players. Place a large bet and all they see are more chips to win - if they get lucky.

Now ALL poker players think this, but most restrain themselves with a degree of common sense. If someone before me raises more than twice the blind, I have to think that maybe my 7 2 won't be good. Well, the Donkey does not consider this and just calls for luck. I love having a Donkey or two at my table - I get most of my chips from them, but you also DO get 'donkeyed', as the saying goes. When there are known donkey's at my table and I have a little luck running with me, you almost can't keep me out of their pots.

True Story

I was visiting the casino with my daughter one day and we were looking at the poker tables. I saw the guy in the small blind look at his cards and I could tell he liked them. I said to her, "Watch this, he will call ANY raise, because he likes his cards."

Everyone folded until there were only the small and big blinds in the hand - the small blind (the man who liked his cards) just calls. The big blind does a four bet. In a Two Dollar game this represents Eight Dollars. The Small Blind does not hesitate to call. The Flop falls and it is all low cards. Small blind checks, big blind does a much larger raise: Forty Dollars. Again, the Small Blind does not hesitate, and calls. The River is a ten, Small Blind checks, the Big Blind then raises Eighty Dollars. Small Blind does not even hesitate and calls.

The River is a Queen. Small Blind checks, Big Blind pushes all in. The Small Blind DOES NOT HESITATE and CALLS the bet. The Big Blind just sits there in shock. The dealer asks him to turn his cards - he is immobile, staring into space. The dealer asks again, he ignores him. Finally the Small Blind turns over K 8 - He has hit nothing and has called the 'All In' with a K as a high card, not even an Ace. The Big Blind pushes his cards into the muck and leaves the table.

Why did the Small Blind call with nothing all the way to the River? Easy: He liked his cards. The guy was an El Primo Donkey - just calling any raise because he liked his cards. The thing is, he was right! Just because someone appears to be stupid does not mean you will beat them. The guy doing the raising was the REAL Donkey, because he didn't read the obvious.

The Donkey is an UNTHINKING player, not a stupid or ignorant one. They do not read the language of betting, they only know when they like their cards.

The message we need to garner from this is not so simple to understand: *IT DOES NOT MATTER HOW WELL YOU PLAY - If you do not read the players correctly on your table, you will LOSE.*

How NOT to be a Donkey

The real message is one of detachment. The superior poker player is an observer of the action, one who is completely involved in the present moment, yet detached from the circumstances surrounding it. Watch carefully the next time you are not in a hand. It is much easier to see what people will do. I knew the Small Blind would call because I was sitting back observing - I was not in the heat of battle.

Big Blind in this story CORRECTLY read that the Small Blind was not strong and believed, in his head, that with enough of a raise they would fold. He was Heads Up, leading the betting, and thought he could buy the blinds. No, the guys calls - OK then, a LARGER raise will buy the pot.

No, Small blind keeps calling. He is calling ANYTHING - and he is calling purely because he likes his cards.

But logic is ruling the Big Blind. He is saying to himself, "He has not hit anything - Surely he will fold to an All In bet on the River!" Mistake number one - *do not presume logic will determine the choices of another player.*

In vast majority of the scenarios you will meet in Poker, the stronger mind wins - But not with Donkeys. They are, bless their cotton socks, only listening to their heart. They fall in love with the most unlikely cards and will not part with them, no matter how hard you bet. They appear to have a immunity to common sense. Donkeys almost never win a tournament, but they take a lot of better players out of the game on a regular basis.

Knowing all the techniques, strategies and theories of Poker counts for nothing when someone just likes their cards and will call any raise. There is no point asking WHY the Small Blind in the earlier example liked his cards, because the answer is simply that he liked his cards.

Don't bother asking WHY the Small Blind called any raise, despite the Big Blind doing everything right. The answer is *he liked his cards*. In other words, he felt lucky. This is, at heart, the calling card of the Donkey - They call anything because they are feeling lucky. And the thing is, occasionally they are right! When you play a Donkey, in any of the many forms they will take, you are playing for luck.

The Psychology of the Donkey

Donkeys, in all their various shades, are in a hand because it gives them a buzz. They LIKE playing with low value cards and beating the guy with QQ or AK and this behavior has been fuelled with online poker. The free games are like cash games without any risk. You lose your 'All In' and you just 'buy back' with all the free chips you have in your bank. Your only penalty is missing the next hand. People have seen how often low value cards "donkey" high value ones and they try and emulate it in a real-life tournament.

Blessed be the God of Donkeys!

As I have said, I want the odd donkey at my table, I get loads of chips from them. What I do NOT want is a Cherry Bomber. The most negative incarnation of the Donkey is called the Cherry Bomber.

So, what IS a Cherry Bomber?

You may well regret asking this question - They are just about the most painful thing you can discover on your table. Even so, they can and do give you a LOT of chips, or you walk home.

The Cherry Bomber

A 'Cherry Bomb' is an irrational large raise or 'All In' SPECIFICALLY where the person doing it does not have the pot odds or the cards to justify the action. This is a valid gambit for stealing a Pot and is often done when you are in the Dealer Position and everyone has just called the Ante. It is a psychological ploy called, 'Punish the Limpers!'.

A *Cherry Bomber* is the person who does this all the time, on one hand trying to scare you out of the pot and steal the chips but on the other just loving the thrill of the risk they are taking with rubbish cards. It is a hybrid combination of Pot Buyer and Donkey.

This type is blind, deaf and dumb to the obvious and will push with any two cards, regardless of the Flop, Turn or River. They rarely ever just call, but randomly raise or push, without any logical reference to the hand they hold. When you RAISE their irrational raises, inside their mind you hear thoughts like, *'He is bluffing' 'He doesn't have cards' 'He is just trying to buy me off'*.

The First Rule with Cherry Bombers: *Logic does not apply.*

The Second Rule is to not try and apply logic, because of Rule One, *Logic does not apply.*

I had AK in one hand. I offered a large pre-flop raise. I get called by a bomber, and the flop shows 10, 8 and 3. I do a follow up raise, twice the pre-flop - I want to see if he has any of that. He pushes back, going 'All In'. Now I just know he has nothing, so I call. He shows J 2 and then hits a Jack on the Turn, taking down the pot. I was curious and asked why he called, let alone raised. I quote you his reply, "I knew you had nothing of that and were just bluffing with high cards!"

Logic, common sense and awareness are not the strong point of Cherry Bombers. If he knew I had high cards, he also knew I was well ahead of him. No, the REAL reason he pushed was to try and buy the pot, hoping I would think he had a ten or similar. Point is, you can do everything right, raise, call and fold at the right times, yet you will still lose a percentage of hands. It is the cost of doing business.

The Cherry Bomber became crystallized in a book entitled, "Kill Phil". It is a technique designed to win hands against professional players - basically, when they raise pre-Flop - push. The principle is simple - the vast majority of professional players will fold to an 'All In' pre-Flop - until you walk into a monster and then soon afterwards you are walking home. While this is a valid technique in certain circumstances, it is akin to throwing a stick of dynamite into the centre of the table and hoping it doesn't explode egg all over your face..

This Cherry Bomber tends to have the attitude, "In for a penny, in for a pound!" You will not find a professional player who wants to be in a hand with them. Because they are fools they cannot be read and so you are in a hand playing purely for luck. You almost never see them at a Final Table - where Cherry Bombing is a valid action - and rarely, if ever, will you see them take down a tournament.

Summary

There are many names we use for Donkeys, but over all they are what we term as "Calling Stations" - people who call bets without the cards to justify their actions. Remember, you are there to win whereas they are there to have fun. When it is no longer fun, they will bomb out of the tournament and go onto the poker machines for the next thrill.

Donkeys are inveterate losers, so welcome them with open arms and bless their little cotton socks. They represent the majority of players, and THESE are the people who will chip you up and get you to the final table. They are also the ones who will send you home early, because you cannot really read what they have. Remember, if you have Donkeys at your table, "Logic does not Apply".

"There's something that happens to people when they see the opportunity to make money. Greed flavored with desperation, especially at a poker table, gives rise to a moment when the eyes change, the humanity vanishes, and the players become bloodthirsty, flat-eyed predators."
Molly Bloom

The POT Buyer

No, this is not the person behind the shed doing deals with illegal dugs. In a game of poker it is the person who regularly tries to buy the pot in front of them. They are easy to pick, and relatively easy to play. After the Donkey, this is the person who will give you the most chips.

So many people hate the pot buyer. In truth, you can get a more chips from them than you do a donkey, because they will call ALL IN pre-flop bets with not very much.

The principle is simple, this person who raises, and raises, to drive you out of the hand. They may have something, they may not, but they just keep raising. This pushes weaker players from the hand even though, when last called, they turned over nothing. When a Pot Buyer chips up, they become the Table Bully - let them get chips, and you will suffer.

You generally Trap Play a Pot Buyer. This is when you have great cards but don't raise them until the river - Even when you have premium cards, you just call their incessant raising. I watched a guy with Pocket Aces just call a Pot Buyer. I got out of the hand with J 10 because I could see the guy to my left smiling to himself. That is a clear clue that he has picked up a monster. I guessed it would be Aces or Kings.

The Pot Buyer in this instance acted predictably - he raised pre-Flop, raised the Flop, raised the Turn, then went 'All In' on the River. He gets called and turns over A 6 - He has hit nothing. The fellow to my left turns over AA and the Pot Buyer is out of the game. Sadly, the hand I folded tripped up and I would have won, but it was the correct call at the time.

You can also out-bid a pot buyer. And with this type, it is not betting, it is purely bidding. It is a 100% auction where the highest bidders wins. A simple and easy technique to put a Pot Buyer on notice is to DOUBLE his raise, no matter what you have, no matter what the flop.

Now the next bit is EXTREMELY important. If he folds, he is a smart Pot Buyer who asked a question, got an answer, then got out of the pot. But look closely at HOW he acts as soon as you double his raise.

Watch his/her eyes as you re-raise their bid for the pot. They will either shrink (in doubt, suspicion, whatever) or gleam. If you see a gleam, he/she either has the goods, or he/she is a mad gambler and you just pushed his/her crazy button. Either way, unless you have the goods, fold to his/her next raise.

If he then checks, that is almost worse because you are left in limbo. Now you have to pick what level of Cherry Bomber is mixed with his Pot Buyer - There is NO Pot Buyer who does not have an inheritance of Cherry Bomber in him or her, which means they are entirely unpredictable. So sometimes the best way to play these people is simply to distract them. Start TALKING, and try and find some sort of read on them. Some games will not let you talk directly to a player unless you are heads up. In this case, talk to the person beside you.

Talking Your Way Through a Hand

There is ONE thing you have in your hand that is your greatest asset, but few people use it - your mouth! Just talking can pay off big time.

In most tournament play, you have to be heads up with a player to start talking directly to them. But even if you are just thinking about your next action, you can chat to the person beside you and ask them if they think the Pot buyer actually has anything. The dealer may instruct you to not talk about the hand you are playing to anyone else, you can then talk to the DEALER and argue that you are making conversation, because it is obvious that the guy raises everything and he can't have the goods all the time. It is not the words, but the distraction you need!

This is super effective with Pot Buyers, because Pot Buyers are attention seekers. They have a huge sign over them that read, "look at me!" So, look at them, ask questions, see how they react.

I have watched professionals talk themselves through the most extraordinary calls or folds. Just talking, watching, perhaps sticking a pin in to see how the opponent reacts - all this gets them OFF the notion of buying the pot and into your hands. Anything you say is purely designed to either heat them up or cool them down - This is your call.

Heating him up: (drive him to act) *"Do you really think anyone on this table believes you have the goods every hand? I know I don't - and I think you are WAY behind here."* Now sit and watch for the reaction. If he boils, he has nothing. So you push. Alternatively, if he asks what you are going to raise, he WANTS you to bet. So you generally Check, saying, "You love to raise - off you go!" or words to that effect.

Cooling him down: (push him to fold) "You know, you HAVE been raising a lot of hands, and I am pretty certain if I go All In there are a whole lot of people who will be interested in what you do. If you fold, as you must, they will all know. If you call, as you want to, they will all know. Bit of a problem for you, yes?"

Flipping the action by making the next choice THEIR problem usually gets some sort of response. Presenting logic like this will give you a clue. Watch his eyes, watch his hands. If he looks happy and his hands go to his chip stack, he has a hand. If he looks happy but his hand DO NOT go towards his chips, he is most likely drawing to a straight, a flush, a whatever. It is anything but a given, but it is often like this. If his eyes don't change much but his hands just go for his chips, he disbelieves you. He/she probably has an Ace and thinks they are good.

If the person sits impassively and gives no reaction, well who knows. One thing is certain, they are NOT Pot Buying. They are possibly a better poker player than you think and YOU may be the schmuck on the table.

In the end, the really massive pots will most often come to you from Pot Buyers. They are betting addicts for whom winning chips is a drug - they just have to keep pushing for more. *'Push, and they will fold!'* is their credo. Eventually you, or someone else on the table, wakes up with a monster - then they will hand over all their chips and the table will laugh as they walk to the exit.

I was in a hand with one of these guys - I had J9 suited. I like these middle suited-connected cards. The Pot Buyer to my right acts with a predictable four times the blind raise. I call. The flop is J 9 nothing. He raises the pot. I just call, I KNOW he will keep raising so I let him to the work. Next card is another 9 - He raises to almost my entire stack.

Inwardly I am laughing, outwardly I am looking hesitant. I was pretty certain I had the nuts, so I don't want to distract him - I want to encourage him. I sigh, saying, "You probably DO have that Nine or that Jack, but no point in just calling, I am All In."

This is the thing, he did not *hesitate* to call the balance. He flips over AK - He still looks confident with his quality pre-flop hand. I flip the full house - his jaw hits the ground - the table then laughs their heads off, so much so that we never see him at the venue again.

Important Note:- *It is a powerful strategy to pause and look someone in the eye when asking them a question. Laugh in their face if you want them to call. Look blankly if you don't.*

The Big Man

The Chinaman, the Texan.

This is the type of player that secretly fears loss of face. They NEED to look good, and will want to play any hand they have high cards. Whether it is because of the pretty girl they have with them, or because they are just arrogant, they will stay and call bets they should fold. These are the people who keep calling because they have hit something or they hold an Ace.

I watched two Chinese guys at a Casino being extremely aggressive in a hand. One would raise, the other re-raise and eventually they were 'All In' at the River. The flop was A K 7 - the turn nothing, the river nothing, yet at every street was a raise and a re-raise. They are BOTH all in and turn over - can you believe - 2 7! They refused to fold because they hit, then they refused to fold because they would look weak. To these people, losing a few hundred dollars is cheap if they look strong.

There is a bit of the "Big Man" in everyone. What's more, it is a valid poker strategy - when you flat all people's raises and stare them down you win the psychological warfare that is Poker. It is amazing how some people won't even SHOW their cards by the river, for fear of losing face. It is ALSO a strategy you can employ to set people up for a fall - Act the Big Man, call their raises, then double their raise, push back. So many will fold to what seems strong resistance.

I had a poker friend (who thought he opened a $20 Red but accidentally opened a TWELVE THOUSAND dollar bottle of Chateau Rothschild one day when I dropped him off, but that is a long story) who had a brilliant strategy. He would look the person raising in the eye, and say, "I am checking this Flop/Turn/River because I want you to bet - but I am letting you know, no matter what you bet, I am calling."

If they made a bet, any bet, he pushed all in, saying, "Sorry, did I say I would call? I meant to say I would go all in." You cannot believe the numbers of players that then fold.

This is a combination of playing the Big Man and combining it with the Cherry Bomber. Did my friend have cards? I have no idea - no one ever called him to find out!

This is a variation of the standard check-raise and, when playing a Pot Buyer or a professional, it is a simple and effective way to get them off a hand. But if you play the Big Man AGAINST another Big Man, it doesn't work. He may just call you thinking his Ace is good! There is no point betting to ask a question with this type - they will call and all you are doing is blindly throwing chips into a pot. This is the HARD part about playing this type of poker player, no answers to your questions - So, how DO we get feedback? You start talking.

The way to deflate the Big Man is to compliment him or her. Simple words like, "I have noticed what a staunch a player you are. You don't fold easy and I respect that." What you say doesn't matter, just lead in with a compliment that is at least half-true. The next part is where you get the read from this type. "Now I am going to make a bet, a respectful bet, because I want to know where you stand with this hand."

Talking your way to the Pot

You may not believe it, but they usually fold unless they DO have cards. Why? They have nothing to prove anymore, you have praised them, shown respect, appealed to the REASON they are there, to be a Big Man. Even if they KNOW this strategy, they will still fold unless they have cards. The hard part - *what do they consider to be cards?*

You need to watch a few hands they are in - Because they call players down you often get to see what they have. If you have a Big Man at a table, stay out of hands with them until you figure their calling range.

The Big Man is in a hand because he has cards he likes. But he is at that table for another reason, and it is not to win. The reason they play is not to LOSE. So many "Big Men" on the poker table are very small men in real life. They will happily spent a few hundred bucks to feel big and important for an hour or two. They are not playing to win, they are playing not to LOSE - Losing self-respect, losing self-esteem, this is a far greater cost to them than losing money.

GIVE them respect, HAND them esteem, and you can control their actions with small bets. Challenge them, and they will call anything. Which obviously means, when you have the nuts you do the *opposite* to complimenting them - You insult their game play. You criticize everything they have done - you bring to mind the call they made with just an Ace that took down the pot - that wasn't a WIN! That was stupidity and you HOPE they will be that stupid in this hand. etc. etc.

I watched a professional gambler do this in a Casino one night. He raised with nothing, saying, "I hope someone has cards they can call with, because I don't want to waste these beauties!" He gets a call from a Big Man. Not a raise, just a call. The flop goes 2 7 4 - absolute rubbish, but with this, the professional starts insulting the guy who called him. "You really don't know how to play this game, do you? You have no idea what you are doing. You are a cakewalk and your only purpose at this table is to give me chips."

The professional keeps raising, the guy keeps calling. On the river, the pro goes all in, the sap calls and flips over JJ thinking he was trap playing and massively ahead. The professional flips 4 7 and takes the pot with two pair. The poor guy with J J is shattered. He has been made to look a fool AND lost all his money. He leaves the table in disgrace.

As soon as he ups and leaves, the pro is back to chatting happily. EVERYTHING he did after the flop was designed to target that player, to make sure they called - he had no personal ax to grind, he just wanted the guys money. The Big Man, on the other hand, was there for the wrong reasons - He needed to LOOK GOOD. But more than this, he wanted to bring the noisy little brat down to size - Vengeance is bad - Anger is bad - They are death to your chips in any game of poker.

Underneath, the Big Man is a whole barrel load full of anger and resentment. Trigger it with insults or control it with compliments and you will beat them easily.

A thing that always makes me laugh, a pretty girl comes to the table, and the "Big Men" there just go to water. They can't play for beans when the eyelids start fluttering at them - Which is why the pretty girl is sitting there with so many chips.

"Whoever coined the phrase 'a man's got to play the hand that was dealt him' was most certainly one piss-poor bluffer."
Jeannette Walls

The Old Woman:

This is the safety player. They only raise pre-flop with AA, KK, QQ or AK and sometimes not even then. They will CALL with cards they like, which could be anything as weak as J 7 off, but they only RAISE pre-flop with high pockets or AK. They are just horribly easy to get chips off.

Obviously, it is just a name - Any super conservative player is an "Old Woman". The thing is, you KNOW what they are raising with, so if you jag two pair on the flop, you can raise and they will call anything. This type rarely, if ever, do HUGE pre-flop raises. They are SAFETY PLAYERS - as a result they often progress deep into tournaments, but they almost never win. Why? Because they play it safe.

Be warned, after the Flop if they have a flush draw or a strong draw, or pockets above the flop, they will call a large raise. It is pointless putting in a massive bet here unless you have trips or better. You play Old Women with nibble bets in order to see how they react. If you think you are good, you nibble (Small ball) to the river. THIS is where you put in a large bet. You are literally fishing for chips against this type of player - if there are no Queens to Aces on the flop and you have two pair, you are usually good.

Question: Is there any point trying to bluff out an Old Woman?

Answer: There is ALWAYS a point in seeking to bluff people off a pot. That is the WHOLE POINT of poker! It is a game of bluff.

The real question is HOW to bluff an Old Woman off the pot. Let's face it, if they have AA they are not folding to any bet, no matter the size. The Old Woman is happy to go home saying they got donkeyed - For them, losing with AA is almost as good as winning the tournament they never win. The answer is that it is not dissimilar to how you play the Big Man - You COMPLIMENT them.

"I know you have raised with AA or KK - I get that. And I want to say, if you hit the Ace of the King you need on the river, you win - But I like you and I really don't want to see you go home early. SO I am making a bet that is easy for you to fold. But if you don't and if you get lucky I will only praise your fortitude. I am All In." Words similar to these have an extraordinary effect on the Old Woman type of player. Unless they have hit trips, or unless they have the most massive draw, they will fold.

Whingers

There are annoying variations of this type, the whinger being one of them. These are safety players who constantly whine about the cards they fold. There are also the complainers, ("You have nothing, I know you have nothing but I have to fold.") and the nervous nellies, who are the type that complain about how people shuffle chips, play with chips, or any one of the standard things most people do with their hands to occupy their minds during the often dull periods between hands.

Cardists

There are also people I call CARDISTS. Just as a racist discriminates according to color of skin, a Cardist discriminates according to the color of their cards. Unless they are both painted, or paired, they want nothing to do with them. The Cardist criticizes other players for calling them with what they call 'rubbish'. The thing is, if you have an Old Woman Cardist, you KNOW what they are playing. You call BECAUSE you know what you are up against, not because of the cards you hold.

We all know AK are great cards to have, but if you raise on them and five people call, and there is no A or K on the flop, you are in trouble. The truth is, I have won more chips with 3 5 suited than AK, AQ, etc.

That said, there is an old saying, *"The race may not always go to the swift, nor the battle to the strong, but it is safer to bet that way."* The key word is SAFER - When you are in a hand where you KNOW the person will play to safety you have a massive advantage over them.

Tournaments are not won in safety. Hands are won, pots are won, but tournaments are won through bold action matched with correct reads, the right type of betting at the right time, and the right folds.

The Cardist is not only biased towards premium cards, they are easily bet off them by people they suspect will call with anything. This is, until they get annoyed, and call your All In out of spite and anger. Which is great if you have the cards!

Playing Known Types

Put an Old Woman, a Big Man, a Pot Buyer and a Donkey on my table, and I will usually have their chips inside a couple of hours. Why? Because they are predictable.

The problem is that in real life, these "types" are not so clear cut. The Old Woman has a little bit of Donkey in them, the Big man has a little bit of Cherry Bomber, etc. We have to determine what percentage of each 'type' we have in any given hand, and it is a bit of a moveable feast - people change over the course of a tournament and over the course of a single hand.

A person who started the tournament as Trap Players but who isn't winning can get tired of their run of no cards and turn into a Cherry Bomber. The safety player can become the Big Man and call any raise. Everyone and everything changes according to their runs of luck.

We will talk about this later, but the simple truth is, luck hits every three to five hours in any given tournament. You will have a run where all is golden and you just keep hitting and winning. The rest of the time it is a grind.

As tournaments run into hours, the grind starts to wear and people lose patience. This is when you begin to see their TRUE colors. You will discover the most ardent Trap Player is really an Old Woman / Donkey / Chaser underneath the controlled surface.

Again, simply talking will break the surface tension and reveal what is hiding in the depths. Friendly banter can change a person's perception and when they see you as a friend, it will cause them to act in very different ways than when they considered you the enemy.

Can I tell you a little secret? *The REAL art in Poker is taking their chips and having them love you.*

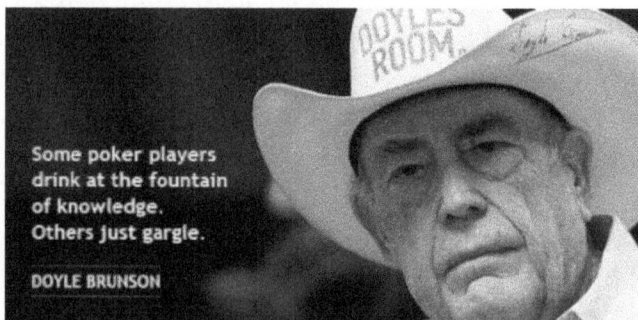

Some poker players drink at the fountain of knowledge. Others just gargle.

DOYLE BRUNSON

The Chaser

CALLING STATION

The Chaser is, as the name implies, a person who chases. In poker, it is a person chasing a card - they call raises in the hope of catching whatever it is they need. Everyone chases to some degree, but intelligent Chasers versus random Chasers are two different animals. The pure blood Chaser is rare and is almost always combined with a bit of Donkey - which is to say, they KNOW you have better cards, but call anyway, for whatever reason they call logic at the time.

A general description of this type is as follows:

A/ Pre-flop: Calls any raise that is less than three times the blind. Calls with almost any cards - they want to see what hits.

B/ On the Flop: Calls any draw. Calls or Re-Raises any flush draw/open ender or situation with Eight or more outs.

C/ On the Turn or River: Calls any three times the blind raise with any pair, regardless of the board

D/ Variation called The Doubter: One who calls any three times the blind raise to the River because they have an Ace or pocket pair, regardless of the board.

The other general term for them is a "Calling Station" because they call for slim odds. At best, Chasers are working on the basis of a 30% chance to win - typically this is a flush draw, straight draw or odds that call for any two cards to win.

The important difference between a person who chases intelligently and the person playing purely for luck is an understanding of odds. Your typical chaser does not even KNOW their odds and just call because they hope to catch their card. A rule of thumb for calling when you haven't hit is very simple: If there are two cards you can hit that will give you the hand, and if the raise equals the pot or under, you have odds to call. If you only have one card to call for, your odds say you can call any raise that is less than 25% of the existing pot.

We will get into odds shortly, but for now let us have a brief look at some examples, because it relates to playing against a Chaser.

Chaser Example ONE

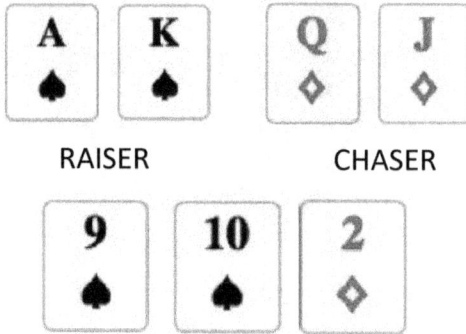

A ♠	K ♠		Q ♦	J ♦

RAISER   CHASER

9 ♠	10 ♠	2 ♦

As Odds go, AK is calling to NINE cards, QJ is calling to EIGHT. But Q J can ALSO hit a Queen or a Jack, which gives another six outs - So while A K is ahead, the chase is for FIFTEEN OUTS.

With TWO CARDS to come, this is more than half the deck. SO, Q J has a good chance of winning!

Playing Your Odds

L et's say you hold Q J with the Flop as described above. There are 6K chips in the pot. The person to your right (with A K) bets 3K - You have landed an open ended straight draw and with a runner runner flush draw. You have EIGHT OUTS - any 8 or K probably picks up the pot. This give you a 30% calling equity.

Your odds are clear: 6K plus 3K Raise = 9K - Calling 3K for 12K with your Q J equals 25% of the pot. You would call.

But let's say YOU have the AK and the person with the QJ is a known Chaser. You KNOW they will call because they have that 'interested' look - Chasers always get this when they want to be in a hand.

So, you go for a 6K raise. The addition is 6K + 6K = 12K - So they want to call, and they do the math - 12K plus their 6K equals 30% of the pot because once they have their chips in, the Pot become 18K!

6K is 33% of 18K so ANY Chaser will call this raise.

A ♠	K ♠		Q ♦	8 ♦		9 ♠	10 ♠	2 ♦

What if they have only ONE card that will secure the hand? Let's say they hold 8 Q - then they need a JACK. Their calling equity plummets to 15% - This SHOULD change everything. But not for our died-in-the-wool chaser. They just know that Jack is coming and the Queen is probably good if it hits as well, so that's two cards to call for!

Let's stick with the 6K raise for now - 15% of an 18K in the pot is only 2700. Calling equity says they must fold - but no proper Chaser will fold.

A ♠	K ♠		Q ♦	J ♦		8 ♠	7 ♠
RAISER			CHASER			CHASER	

9 ♠	10 ♠	2 ♦		10 ♦	8 ♥
				CALLER	

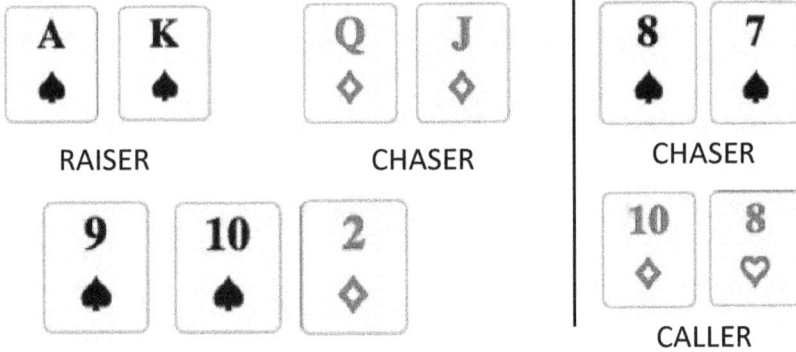

Chaser Example THREE

Surprisingly: As Odds go, everyone has fairly even chances to win

L et's say you hold A K with three others in the pot. Everything changes when there are more people in a hand. Let's go back to the original example and add 8 7 Spades and 10 diamonds and 8 hearts. You hold A K and are choosing to raise 6000 into a 6000 pot.

8 7 is angling for the flush draw AND a straight AND a straight flush - they aren't folding. 10 8 has HIT and is ahead! Q J has an open ended straight draw, they aren't folding. NOW you have three people calling, which means with a 6K raise into a 6K pot and THREE PEOPLE calling you get: Four x 6K + 6K Pot = 30K. Everyone has a 30K pot to call for. Not ONE person is folding here.

You, with the A K, are now in a hand CHASING a Spade, a King or an Ace. Even worse, two of your spades will give 7 8 spades a straight flush. Add to this the fact that the solitary TEN is ahead of everyone, and you start to wake up to the notion that it might be better to check this.

Think about it, you KNOW the Chaser with call. With so many people in the hand, there is almost NO bet you can make to get them out of it, so why try? You are putting yourself into maximum risk while your odds for winning are greatly reduced.

When you are in a multi-way hand with a Chaser, all they see is more chips they can win with every raise. Normally you would push 'All In' on the Turn, but no one is leaving this pot - If you do a large bet they are emotionally and financially invested, you are now ENCOURAGING them to call. This is the opposite reason of WHY you bet.

You CAN check it down and see if you pick up the flush or a high card.

How Best to Deal with a CHASER

You need to treat the Chasers on your table more like a math problem than a person. Let's say you land an Ace with AK in the hand and A 5 7 on the flop. You raise a LOT, they call - What are they likely to hold? It could be a straight draw, maybe they hit a card, hit two pair or even hit trips? You just don't know and whatever you raise, they are calling. The ONE thing you know is that the person likes to Chase and that they are probably calling for a 30% chance to pick up a second pair, or a straight, or a whatever.

When you have a chaser in you Pot there is little point thinking about calling equity, pot odds, pot value or anything most poker players consider. The Chaser will call pretty much anything because they want to catch a card. But there is ONE bet they will rarely call if they haven't hit - the All In on the Turn. And yet, they still might .

I have seen the most unbelievable calls from Chasers. In one hand, two players to my right had already gone All In. When I fold they expose cards forgetting there is another in the hand. The flop is Q J 6 - one shows pocket sixes - he has trips, the other has Q J, two pair. The last player thus gets to see their cards - and HE STILL CALLS with A K.

There is only one card that can save him, a ten, and he bet his tournament on drawing to one card, despite the obvious fact he was massively behind. Guess what, he got his ten! Now THERE is a dedicated, died-in-the-wool Chaser.

You may want to blame the Chaser for his bad play, but really, it is like blaming an addict for their addiction.

If the two-pair guy had pushed ALL In on the TURN, the Chaser might have folded. Why? He is chasing for a single card - but if he gets it all in on the flop, he sees he has TWICE the chance of hitting his ten. This is how Chasers think, or not think, as the case might be. When they sees the turn and knows there is only one chance, most Chasers stop running after a card and fold. It was the push from under the gun with the two pair that pulled the Chaser *into* the call. How can anyone call to such slim odds? Easy to understand when you get the psychology.

This type do not want to WIN so much as feel LUCKY. The thrill of the chase, the sense of Lady Luck being with them - THIS is what they want. That Chaser got given the ultimate thrill - hunting down two pair and trips to score the ONE card he needed.

Too Many Chasers on a Table is Bad

I love having ONE chaser at a table, I am very careful with two, but hate having three or more. Why? Odds - Chasers are generally running to 30%. But the real Chasers DO NOT SEE percentages, odds, or anything but the thrill of the chase and a hope that luck is with them. But because you DO see the odds, oddly enough, (pun intended) this puts you at a disadvantage.

Let me frame this for you. Three Chasers with a 30% Call Equity each adds up to 90% OVERALL Negative Equity to you. Does this make sense? They still have their individual calling odds, but it is now all of them against you. Odds are curious creatures, but any fool can work out that three people angling to catch something is harder to beat than one.

This 90% Negative Equity is not based on fixed and accurate odds. It is meant as a general outline to give you a sense of what Chasers represent in any given hand.

Yes, you are putting out nibble bets, you are asking questions to see if you ARE ahead, but if your nibbling tells you the two chasers have 30% each, then just 40% to YOU is not good. One up with the chaser and you are at 70% positive - This is where the 'good' starts.

However, if you flop the Nutz, you want all the Chasers in the world to call and give you a massive chip up.

Chasers test your ability to read what they have, what they are after, and how well you sit in any given hand. If you have ONE Chaser, you are probably good. Two or more, it is a dangerous hand to be in. But that said, they still have to catch a card.

Here's a little secret: When I have more than one chaser in any given hand, I do small bets and watch. ALL Chasers get a look in their eye when they catch their card.

Why does this happen? Chasers are essentially greedy pigs. They inherently want more than their fair share and when they get it they give a signal. You can hide emotions, mask your face, wear dark glasses to obscure your pupils - but when a Chaser catches their card, they give a little leap inside. Hitting luck is the REASON they play! Most people do this, but Chasers give a stronger reaction. OBSERVATION and careful betting wins against Chasers!

Remember - *Folding is a win when you are behind.* SAVING chips is as good as winning them.

Betting and Calling Equity

There is one great rule in poker - Bet when you are ahead. The idea is to bet hard NOT see a River - But a Chaser wants to see a River more than any other card. The thing is we ALL want to chase to get the card we need, but how MUCH will be call to bets that challenge our chase?

We include this little snip to start to give you an idea of what we call CALL EQUITY - or VALUE to CALL.

POKER PUZZLE: How Much CALL EQUITY?

A ♥	5 ♣	A ♣	8 ♥	8 ♣	7 ♣

Any Ace - No
Any Five - Yes
Any Queen - Split
4 OUTS to WIN
4 OUTS to SPLIT

Any Ace - Yes
Any Eight - Yes
Any Queen - Split
8 OUTS to WIN
4 OUTS to SPLIT

Any Club- Yes - 9
Any Nine - Yes - 3
Any Seven - Yes - 3
15 OUTS to WIN

K ♦	10 ♣	J ♣

The Flop poses the question: *How much does the leading hand have to bet to get the others out of the Pot?*

8 7 clubs is the weakest hand yet it has the most opportunity to win. Fifteen OUTS over the two cards = Thirty OUTS = 60%.

But A 8 is still ahead. The pot is 6000. Calling Equity poses the question: *How MUCH does A 8 have to bet to get 8 7 out of the hand?*

Well, 3600 is 60% of 6000 so a bet over this would work, yes? NO!

You add the bet PLUS the call into the pot THEN work out the Calling Equity. The answer is there is almost NO bet that will get 8 7 out on this flop. Bet 6000, add that to the 6K Pot to get 12000. The 8 7 with its 6K Call makes it an 18000 Pot. 6K is one third of 18K - An EASY Call.

Bet 20K and the call makes the pot 46K - a 43.5% Call into a 60% value. An 'All In' that puts their tournament at risk is the only bet here.

The Trap Player:

This is the most dangerous player on any table. The general understanding is that these people DO NOT raise with good cards. They wait for a raise hoping to catch a pot buyer, cherry bomber, etc. They are, as the name says, laying a trap for inexperienced players to walk into. But a REAL Trap Player is not a spider who waits for the perfect hand then allows everyone to bet into them. REAL Trap Players set up scenarios whereby other players feel they are ahead, or can get ahead.

As a basic outline, Trap Play involves only a limited number of cards pre-Flop. AA, KK, or QQ - AK or AQ. To a far lesser degree small pockets and Suited Connected cards are used. Each is played differently. Let's run a few obvious plays, to get an idea how Trap Play works.

Scenario One: The Nutz on the Flop

Now, the most obvious and the one everyone hopes for is when you check the nuts on the flop. This generally means a Straight Flush or Quads down to a Full House. It is common sense to not raise anyone out of a hand when you want them in and betting. Classic scenario, you hit a straight Flush with 4 6 of Hearts - 3 5 7 of Hearts are the flop. You almost cannot be beaten - someone would have to have 8 9 hearts and pick up 10 J hearts to win.

No one in their right mind raises, do they? Wrong. You should be asking questions and in this case you physically ask a question with a small raise, "Anyone have a heart?" Why do I do this? Every man and their dog know that someone with the nuts checks the flop, so I CAN'T have a straight flush, can I? First Principle in Trap Play: *You trap through misdirection, not just by waiting for someone to bet.*

Anyone who calls a small raise almost certainly has a heart, or they have two pair, or maybe a straight. Now you know what level of INTEREST is in a hand, you can start to lay the Trap. The bait is the Pot! So you need to encourage people to increase the size of the Pot.

This is the reason you are trapping - you give people the chance to chase what they need. Just waiting till someone bets is a bad idea. You do not get chips by passively waiting, you get them by actively encouraging betting.

The way you do this depends on the types of Poker Players in your pot. If you have pot buyers, they will actively re-raise your small raise - but only if they pick you for NOT being a Trap Player. Any Chaser will call a raise that is less than three times the blinds if he/she has a high heart in their hand. The Donkey will call almost anything by way of a minimum raise. The Old Woman needs to have a picture card as a heart to call. The Big Man will call with any pair over the flop or any heart, or even AK with NO hearts.

The Professional Player will make their choice based on who they pick to be in the hand. If they have a high heart they will call. So what has your small raise done for you? You have QUALIFIED the table - if you have read your poker types correctly, you can almost pick what cards the people who are calling you have. Your very BEST scenario is that if there is another Trap Player at the table and they just call you. They have Ace-whatever of hearts and are thinking they are baiting YOU.

There are so many variations of how to play this sort of hand, but let's say ALL these types call your small raise. No-one has re-raised you - What do you do on the Turn? Well, with so many calling ONE raise, you have an excellent opportunity to increase the pot. Another small raise, double the blind is usually ideal. Keep in mind the size of the pot by now. Let's say they are 1K blinds. You had six players in the hand, so 6K in the pot before the flop. You bet another 1K on the Flop with everyone calling, that's 12 K in the pot.

Let's say you now bet 2K. If they called 1K they are calling 2K - Why? After your raise, there is 14K in the pot. 2K represents 15% equity. EVERYONE has 15% in their minds and that fat juicy pot gets them going. If the Pot Buyer holds an A or a K of hearts, they will re-raise you. If the trap player holds a Flush with the Ace, they will be tempted to start shutting the door, trying to stop someone lucking the straight flush that is self-evident. The Donkey just calls hoping to hit whatever they need, the Chaser will most likely call. Most Professionals will drop out unless they hold the Ace Hearts or a flush.

Before the River hits it is best to look vulnerable and weak. Cultivate a "hope for the best" look. It's true, you ARE hoping for a massive re-raise. Let us presume everyone calls your 2K - that puts 24K into the pot. Last to act before the River hits may well try their luck at stealing the pot. Bets practice is to just call a raise and look like you need a favorable River - You DO, but not in the way they are thinking.

When the River comes, no matter what it is, you check. Another heart means the person with the Ace will bet hard, so you don't need to raise. If there is no Heart, the Pot Buyer will try and steal. The Trap player who had Ace-whatever of Hearts will push. You have a huge pot set up for the taking and the only bets coming back to you will be large ones.

Whatever the bet, when it is your turn to act, just double it. You can even vocalize your doubts, "Sorry, don't believe you." or similar.

Even as I say this, I know every hand is different - What I suggest is merely this, a suggestion, but one based on an averaging of the untold thousands of hands I have played. Please note - You will rarely catch a GOOD player out with any of these tricks and the very best of them know and understand trap play. If a good player picks what you are doing, they will find a way to use it AGAINST you.

Scenario Two: Big Cards

Scenario One is extremely rare. The most likely story with trap play is that you will have Aces or Kings and you just call with them. Someone else in the hand has two cards they like, and they raise. Once more, you do NOT sit passively and just call. Once there is action, once someone is interested in their hand, you Re-Raise. Trap Play is NOT sitting there passively, it is waiting for an opportunity to maximize a return on investment.

What you do next is dependant on the number of people in the hand, or likely to come into it. A simple rule of thumb is to multiply the raise by the number of people in the hand. Heads up, just double, one prior caller to the raise means three times the raise. If you think the person to your right is eager to get in, four times the raise. If EVERYONE is reaching for chips and calling, you have a decision to make. Call, push or fold. Remember: Aces against four other players are NOT strong.

A basic poker principle: If you cannot make a raise that will lessen the number of callers, don't raise. You might raising to increase the size of the pot pre-Flop, but mostly you raise to lessen the number of hands in play. Trap play ONLY WORKS when you have minimized the number of people in a hand, OR you are calling a hand cheaply.

The reality is that with three or more people in a hand, no pre-flop cards are strong. If more than two people call, there is a significant likelihood that two of them hold an Ace and you have no way of improving your hand. Trap Play is dependant on the number of callers. I have witnessed one hand where there was a raise under the gun, another raise, and another before it came to the dealer. He was holding Aces, the rest of the table held 44, 77 and JJ. The guy with the Aces recognized his All In would meet with everyone calling, so he just called.

Everyone just calls the last raise and the Flop falls - I kid you not - 4 7 J. Under the gun pushes, everyone calls. ALL the small pockets have hit trips, while the guy with the Aces presumes someone has jagged something - but what can he do? He calls and the River turns up the Ace he needs. Luck saved him, not skill, but better lucky than smart.

The message is simple, four people in a hand exponentially reduces the chances of Aces or Kings holding up. Sure the small pockets have only 20% equity to win, but 4 players with 20% = 80%. Heads up, you are at 80% with Aces. Four up, you are at 20% - roughly equal for everyone on the table. I know it sounds crazy, but that is the math. We will look at this more closely on the section on Odds.

Scenario Three: Suited / Connected

When you hold J 10 suited, 8 9 Suited, etc it requires a specific sort of trap play. You ideally RAISE the hand if you are going to Trap Play it in this case. You have high percentage cards, so you need to minimize the number of hands in play and you need to make it look like you are holding gold. Trapping is NOT passive - it is actively painting a picture.

How you proceed is entirely dependant on the table image you have created. If people believe you are a solid player, they will be folding K 9 and Q 8 - precisely what you need OUT of the hand. You might even get Ace Rag out - No matter what the flop, if you have raised pre-flop you need to reach for chips and be prepared to raise again.

"What?" you exclaim! "This is not Trap Play - It is Pot Buying!"

Correct, but no one will suspect your actions, because prior to this you have shown NO Pot Buying tendencies. This is a very different sort of Trap Play, trapping WITHOUT cards. You are trapping their MINDS. You are convincing them they are behind based on your previous actions. If someone raises massively before the betting comes to you, fold. The trick here is to LOOK like you are ready to raise.

Scenario Four: AK / AQ or small pockets

Various other scenarios are when you are holding AK or AQ. or small pockets. You are simply calling a raise to see a flop when you are acting as a Trap Player - This is the traditional Trap Play, don't raise, see the flop and, if favorable, work from there. Traditional Trap Play has you hitting trips and checking - You are waiting for someone to hit a card.

If Scenario Four is all you do in your Poker Life, you will rarely win a tournament. True Trap Play is all about creating scenarios, not living inside them, and maximizing return with workable flops.

I had a guy on a table who folded to every raise I did after the Flop, until in one hand he called. I had AQ and there was A Q 4 on the Flop. I asked him, "You have folded every hand I have raised, yet you are calling this one? I wonder why?" I proceeded to let the cards run out, he kept checking it down as well. He turns over pocket fours, he had trips on the Flop.

This is NOT Trap Play. He should have doubled my raise on the flop - I would have called. If he kept betting the min raise, I would have called - I had two pair! Trap Play is about MAXIMIZING RETURN, and sitting passively will rarely do this. The guy was so obviously dressed up as what he thought was a Trap Player that he became easy to read.

Summary

Playing a professional Trap Player is never easy. You do not get feedback on bets, you never know where you stand, and they are not baited into conversations like most other players. Flopping a full house on the flop and checking it down is not trap play, you might be trapping, but you are not PLAYING the trap.

Trap Play, or slow Play as some call it, is a sophisticated psychology that creates the illusion in the players mind that they are ahead of you when they are not.

I get annoyed at watching commentators speaking of a leading player 'trapping' someone when all they did was wait till the other guy bet, and they pushed back. The other person KNOWS it is either a trap, or a bluff, and are only calling to see if it the latter. This is VERY different from a person believing they are ahead and betting.

It is very hard to beat a proper trap player because you never realise you are behind until the trap shuts on you.

The Professional:

This Professional mixes up all varieties of poker player and chooses who to be in any given hand. There are four major "phases" or categories, but every Professional employs one or more of these in any given hand.

- A/ **The Rock:** By the book player that raises with two high cards, re-raises the flop, and keeps raising until he feels he is behind. If he feels behind, he then checks to river.
- B/ **Bet to Discover:** This type of Player raises to get a read. This is part of the first category, but this is the specific reason WHY the Professional raises - to get a read.
- C/ **Small Baller:** Comes into any cheap pot and drives out weaker players with nibble bets. This is how Professionals chip up in tournaments, taking constant small pots while, in doing so, create angst and hatred from players who then act irrationally.
- D/ **Position Player**: Always calls (and often raises) when they are on or before the dealer button. If the flop is checked to them, they will look to steal the pot.

These are people who have played lots of hands, read all the poker books, and generally play based on the read of the people in front of them. For the most part, they can, but they often have one great weakness - they tend to think they are pretty good.

The overall trick to beating Professionals is to look insignificant, nervous and not particularly bright. My son went into a casino one evening and played the local yokel. He looked at his cards and said out aloud, "So, if you got two kings in this game, that's a good start hand, yes? How much should I bet - $20?"

He bets the twenty and everyone folds. "Hey, this is easy. Let's get more cards!" He didn't have Kings, of course. All the people that thought they were so good sitting there were laughing at how stupid he was - while he was taking their money off them.

Playing the fool is a very valid strategy. Looking at cards, frowning, saying things like, "Gee mister, you must have a great hand to be betting so much. Having all the same suite is good though, isn't it? I think I had better raise, in case you get better."

Stupid crazy stuff like that puts off the Professional and drives them completely looney tunes - particularly when they finally push and find you DO have the cards. Whatever you do to counter the Professional, the goal is to put them out of their rhythm. These people like to control a table, control the betting, and generally punish weakness.

There are three things the Professional is wary of - but you must use these techniques sparingly. The FIRST is written up in the book "Kill Phil". Here you check, then, when the Pro raises thinking you are weak, you go, "All In!". No Professional player likes to be all in pre-flop - unless he has Queens or better he does not have the equity to call. If he DOES call with Ace Rag, he's feeling lucky or is a pretend Professional.

The SECOND is the INVITATION TO RAISE, "I will check and let you raise, yes?" However you do this, you look directly at the guy who is always raising with good cards and invite him to put in chips. If he does, smile and look incredibly pleased. Just double the raise, and see how he reacts. If he re-raises he generally has A Q or better, or he thinks you are bluffing. A re-raise means you must either fold or push. If you call, you are dead unless you get lucky.

One friend, who had made a FORTUNE in Paris with Poker, always pinned people who thought they were Professionals, saying, "I know you want to raise, but I want to let you know, I will be calling any raise you make. Are you raising now?" then he would reach for his chips.

A small note, professional players "Small Ball" when on or near the dealer button. They know how to nibble bet and get other players off balance. If you are in a hand WITHOUT the goods, they sense it and keep nudging till you fold. They are not playing cards, they are playing psychology - they are there to psyche you out, and you have to be incredibly strong-willed and confident to go head to head and win. ALL these suggested techniques are designed to reverse this psyche-out process and dump it back on them.

The THIRD technique is call "Mirror Ball". You reflect everything they do, but in a scattered way. It's a little bit like the "Local Yokel". Whatever they bet, you vocalize what you think they have, "Wow, you must have AK to be betting out as strong as you are - but I can beat that!" - Or words to that effect - Then you re-raise their raise.

Always let the Professional act first - Appear passive and let your words do the battle for you. You are reflecting their type of play, but in a random and scattered way. Professionals look for patterns of behaviour and by just being a bit of a loose cannon, verbalizing that you are good, and betting like you are, puts them off their game. Get it? Their game is to bounce you about, so you BE the bouncing ball, and they have to play catch up.

Once you get these people get off their sense of dominance, you discover the vast majority of them are weak and insecure. Everything they do is really a counter to their own fears and doubts - they have just learned to reverse this and use the negative patterns of others to their advantage. They are not REALLY Professionals, they are just pretending.

Please remember this - ALL players suffer a fear of loss. Loss of chips is one thing, but loss of face, loss of control, these are also real fears that dictate a persons actions. Tournament play is strongly focused on fear as a control measure - Why? If you lose your chips you can't re-buy. Cash games not so much - you lose chips, you buy more.

To control ANY player, but most especially the Professional, you need to lever their FEAR. This is why playing drunks is so difficult, they have no fear and make large, irrational bets - they are like a cherry bomber on steroids but worse, because they BELIEVE they are playing tight and controlled poker, and are working you for a READ - But that read is always that they will be good by the River.

Beware the Beer Goggles

Beer Goggles convince ugly men they look handsome and make lonely old women look young. They also make every other poker player at the table inferior to their great poker prowess. Saying this, beware the Professional who pretends to play like a drunk. And most especially beware the happy chatty "Texan" who is constantly smiling, chatting and complimenting everyone at the table. They are evil creatures, the spawn of Satan himself.

All this said, if you come across a REAL Professional, the only thing that will save you is Luck. When you are dealing with people who make a living from reading other players, you are really playing a relentless machine - one that WILL wear you down and take all your chips unless you happen to walk into a monster hand at just the right time. These people are detached observers of the game - they make no emotional investment, do not suffer fear or insecurity, and are terminators of the table. These are the Detached Observers.

The Detached Observer:

I f you are any good at math, you might be asking a simple question here. "Hey, he said there were only Seven Types of Poker Player - Yet this is the EIGHTH!" I would respond that the EIGHTH player is really all the previous ones rolled into on. This player uses any combination of all the various types according to the people they meet in any given hand. They bring a winning attitude along with skill and perception to any hand they choose to play.

This type of player cares more about position than the cards they hold. Position, pot value, and who they pick as weak playing in the hand are their 'real' cards. They choose any one of the aforementioned types to act out and will do so at random according to circumstance. You cannot get a proper read from them, you will never know what they hold, and you will ALWAYS be betting or calling in the dark when one of these players is at your table. Luck is the only thing that beats them.

- A: This type do not get emotionally involved
- B: Each hand is a new hand
- C: The past does not control their present
- D: Their position at the table and the players on it determine choices more than cards
- E: Watches for patterns of cards and patterns of behavior

You can tell them by the way their gracious acceptance of a loss equals their casual acceptance of a win. This sort of player is best summed up in the little known proverb on the Temple of Apollo at Delphi, a saying that has been there for thousands of years - "Nothing too much". It is where "Moderation in Excess" comes from, but it doesn't really mean this. It really means NOTHING in excess - Not too much happiness, too much grief, too much joy, nor too much sadness. In other words, be tight with emotions.

This attitude is the rock upon which you can build your Poker Church. This is the player who gives no signals that mean anything overmuch to anyone. It is also the person who can fake pupil dilation, a flick of the mouth, whatever they want. When someone achieves true mastery of this state, they become the river that drives the wheel.

When you are in this state of consciousness, for it IS a way of BEING, not thinking, you can almost say with certainty what every other player in your hand has. How? I don't know - you just know. But I will say the obvious here - it is not luck that has the same players at final tables in championship matches, over and over again - Detached clarity is a skill. You need some luck, we cover this in the next chapter, but more hands are won with a correct read then are won with good Pre-Flop cards.

Consider the times when you have been in a hand but folded to a large raise. Now you are sitting back, watching. You look at the two people going heads up and for some reason it is now much easier to read their tells. You can guess much better when someone is bluffing. Why? Because you are NOT INVOLVED. It is so much easier to pick up the subtle signals when you are not caught up in the story.

This is only half the tale, however. You have to mimic the sense of just observing while in the hand, but you ALSO have to mirror back to the person you are up against with a persona or 'type' that works best in this situation. This takes a tremendous LACK of need. You have to genuinely not NEED to win that hand. You must genuinely not NEED to impress the other player, or make them feel less, or make yourself feel superior, or even desire to 'win' - despite the fact everything they DO is to win - The truly detached player becomes *vulnerably invulnerable*.

The **Detached Observer** is extremely sensitive to the currents on a table. It is not an insulated state where you feel nothing, quite the opposite - you feel everything. You let go of your attachment to outcomes, not your connection to the present moment and, because of this, your sensitivity to the shifting sands of fortune is far greater.

Magic happens when you let go. So many times a player will disguise their reactions, but you FEEL a little jump as they see a card turn. They wanted to see that card and you FELT it. Once you get to this degree of sensitivity, it is a powerful assistance in making decisions. It is now a matter of determining what that player believes is 'good'.

I flopped a straight in one hand and the guy to my right literally started tapping his hands in joy. There were three hearts there and he puts in a min bet. Now, you might immediately think he had the flush and your straight is no good - But I had the K hearts and felt NO-ONE could be that stupid to give off such an obvious signal, so I pushed all in.

He calls and turns over the Ace High flush. I was guilty of being attached to my little straight. With three hearts on a table and no Ace of Hearts I should have been testing the waters, not pushing.

Do you want me to call?

It might seem a cliché' but you will hear it on many poker tables - a person pushes, everyone folds, then the last to act asks a very simple question, "Do you want me to call?"

How different it would have been if I had stopped my MIND and just talked to the guy, to see and feel his true thoughts. All I had to do was comment, "You seem so happy I am guessing you landed a flush, but I still have a lot to call for here - Did you want me to raise?" It is simply amazing how people betray their true thoughts and feeling with a simple question. But I didn't, and I lost.

Do you want to win chips and take home prize money? You have to gather ALL the strategies I have previously suggested and talk a person through a hand like they are an old friend, or an old enemy. Act friendly and listen to the response. Act as if you care, but not much.

Yet, at the same time, you have a burning desire to win. Doesn't seem to add up, does it? This is why being a detached observer is so effective, no one can quite add up the sum of your parts and come to anything that makes sense. You are not just ASKING questions, your demeanour is PUTTING questions into people's minds.

Consider this, you have done a big raise and the person to your left smiles quietly, then sincerely asks you if you want them to call. In 'your' world, you are experiencing many emotions. You might have AA or you might have one huge bluff, but the person to your left seems unconcerned by the raise and is simply asking if you want them to call.

Now, you might imagine that a person holding AA says "Yes please!" but they are not that stupid. The CORRECT answer with high pockets is "I DO want someone to call, but not the whole table." Yet hardly anyone ever says that - most people are attached to the hand and they react to this question. They can break out in a sweat (I have seen it often) which for most is a signal to call. They might reach to cover their mouth, an instinctive sign they are lying, or they might be faking this tell.

What they cannot cover up is their first emotional response. Unless they are loaded up with Beta Blockers, they will give off SOME sort of signal because your question is pulling them OUT of their mind and putting them INTO the present moment.

If you feel they are weak, keep asking questions - see if they crack. I use words to the effect: *"I mean, you probably had a better hand pre-Flop - but mine was very playable and I have a lot more chips than you. So, what I am really asking is if you are happy to go heads up and risk the tournament, because for me it is no great issue either way."* Then the magic killer question: *"**What do you want me to do**?"*

Get yourself into the Driving Seat

The whole idea is that YOU are in the driving seat, yet you are telling them that THEY are in the driving seat. You are apparently putting the rudder into their hands and asking them where they want to go.

Here is the hard part. The smart player will say, "I would prefer if you folded. I am happy to take the pot." I would tend to read that as strong - But if you hear, "I don't care either way, call or fold" or reckless words to the effect of, "No guts no glory" - the player is weak. Simply repeating what they say, whatever they say, is usually when you get a true sign of where they are at.

If he seems strong, re-question. *"You are happy to just take the pot?"* If he just nods, he probably has a pair or AK/AQ.

If he seems weak, echo his words. *"No Guts no Glory, hey?"* If he looks like a rabbit in the spotlight, frozen in place, he is scared. If he looks right back at you, he is daring you to call - which could mean he is weak, or covering up his AA. If you do not get a definitive read, ask more questions. You are detached from the outcome, you have played thousands and thousands of heads up hands, this is just another one.

If they stare at me, or look like a frozen rabbit, i might say words to the effect of, "Oh, you have nothing at all?" Eventually they give a strong reaction and you will have to decipher what it means. But consider the other end of the spectrum, the player is detached, they have gone "All In" and said, "I would like ONE caller, not the whole table" to your question.

You have echoed, "You want ONE caller?" and he/she just looks at you then asks in return, "Are you wanting to call?"

What does it mean? You have no idea. Nil reaction, no specific emotional charge to read, you are shooting at a pig in a poke to call. It is very hard to call an All In when you can get no read from a player. If you want to win chips, YOU have to be that player.

Section Two

Prayers to the Gods of Poker

- Respecting Luck

- Recognizing the Energy Flows at a Table

- Understanding how to Create and Capitalize on Opportunity

LUCK and the Poker Gods

*"**Poker** is a combination of **luck** and skill. People think mastering the skill part is hard, but they're wrong. The trick to **poker** is mastering the **luck**."*   Jesse May:

A famous Phil Hellmuth quote goes, *"If there weren't luck involved, I would win every time."* This is true for most professionals - they have learned about timing, mastered the nature of the psychic warfare that is Texas Holdem, and gotten detached enough from the game to get a reasonable read on what sort of cards opponents are holding. This ability is both natural and trained, but once honed it will beat the amateur every time - except for luck.

Even so, there is a reason why the SAME NAMES keep appearing on the final table of major tournaments - this it is NOT Luck. But learning to PLAY your luck, and more importantly, to negotiate OTHER people's luck is essential if you are to win.

As a general rule - in any given tournament, luck will come your way every four hours or so. It is a real thing, everyone gets some. It may run for thirty hands, it may run for one, but there ARE winning streaks. Real luck is not getting Aces - it is having Aces when someone has Kings and wants to raise into you. Even then, they still have twenty percent to hit their card! If luck is not running with you, this is what happens. I have had Aces against AK and the guy bets in. He hits the King on the flop and pushes. I call his all in - laugh when I see his jaw drop as I turn over Aces, only to watch him jag another king on the turn.

Pre-Flop you must IGNORE ODDS - OMG Sacrilege! No one will ever tell you this, but in moment to moment decisions, ignore them. Play the player, play their luck, play with your instincts but most importantly, play to see a flop. Your greatest chance to win any hand is on the Flop! This is the FIRST TIME you have a full poker hand represented.

NO ONE HAS WINNING CARDS PRE-FLOP. Chisel this into your consciousness: *In Texas Holdem, there are no cards that cannot be beaten before a flop is seen.*

The Flop represents pure, unadulterated LUCK. After the flop, you play for the POT ODDS.

This is the primary reason why we MUST observe luck as an important facet of the game. Here you watch for patterns. We notice how cards are working for one person, yet not for another, etc. *I have called All In bets from an unlucky player with garbage cards based PURELY on the fact that they have been unlucky.* Yes, we assess the players, we pick what type they are, we Small Ball the ones we can - but when you are running against luck, NO skill you possess can win. And why play against someone full of Luck?

It pays to pay attention to luck. It runs in certain cards you will hold, it runs in certain players at certain times. It also stops running in all of the above, so it is important to watch and learn the tempo of every table. The three basic rules:

- Never trust luck
- Never play for luck
- Never play against a lucky player.

Everyone has their share of luck, but the Poker Gods are not fair nor do they hand out luck evenly. If the person betting in ahead of you is being lucky, fold unless you can raise them out of it. And a secret: Someone at your table will ALWAYS be running lucky and, if you challenge them before their run ends, they will have your chips.

Mastering the element of luck is the most difficult thing to achieve in poker. Bad luck seems to dog some people - I consider myself one of the unluckiest players, but BECAUSE of this I am keenly attuned to the element of Luck and how it is playing on a table.

I cannot count the number of times I have been heads-up, well ahead of my opponent, and worked them into a position where they have so much in the pot that it is almost impossible for them to fold. I go all-in, they call - still needing a card to beat me. Against all the odds, they get that card. Luck ignores what odds would say.

Bad Beat Story: I had a player in a hand where the flop ran: A A 10 - I have AK, he has 10 9 - This is a tremendous, almost unbeatable position and what is more, I know the player! They have hit they will not fold. So I do a large raise - normally a bad play when you are super strong, but as mentioned, I know the player. I bet half my stack. He calls without hesitation. The Turn comes with another 10!

He shouts "All in!" Even when I call and show Aces over Tens, he still thinks he is winning with his Tens over Aces. And guess what? The River is another Ten. He jags quad Tens and I walk. The odds? The square root of two for him to get running tens.

When it comes down to luck, you can FORGET ODDS!

How do some people appear to defy mathematics? We call it luck, but it is really a combination of many things. Intuition, stupidity, stubbornness - it can all roll up into one big Luck Duck. You can call it dumb luck, beginners luck, bad luck, donkey luck - but whatever you call it, the message is simple - Luck cannot be beaten. *"I would rather be lucky than smart"* as the saying goes.

This defies what a lot of people want to believe. They WANT to hold that aggression and skill will win the game, and they do - but not when they are running against luck.

All the above is purely to stress the absolute GOLDEN RULE of all Poker. *"Do not play against luck!"* If you have a player on your table who is getting lucky beyond all odds, you have to swallow your pride and accept that for this period of time, the Poker Gods are with them.

Conversely, when luck is NOT running for you, your game has to be a scavenger game. You have to play to presumed weakness and raise in a way to create a fold. But if there are smart players on the table, they will see that luck has not been with you and they WILL call. Your luck, if any, is to have not so bright players on your table.

So here is where you make luck work for you - Observe the UNLUCKY PLAYERS at your table, and be sure to be in hands where they are raising. Please remember this simple wisdom: *You will win a lot more hands if you play against unlucky players!* Conversely, you lose a lot less when you accept the tides of fortune are running for the lucky ones.

I have won a lot of tournaments and I can say with certainty that NONE of them had me hitting cards the entire night. We DO have bursts where things fall our way - Recognizing these tides, working with them, this is how we discover the new world.

Note: There are time when the tide never turns - there are nights when the card run out wrong and to pick up a hand you have to bluff, bluff and bluff again. But as I say, tread carefully because astute players who have seen your bad beats will call - not because they have cards, but because you have been unlucky. (Another reason to not see a river)

But you CAN play against Luck. It is a high wire act with no safety net, but it can be done. Essentially you have to paint a picture in the mind of the lucky player where they do NOT want to call when you push to grab a pot. I will describe an actual tournament where this happened.

How to play AGAINST Luck and WIN

In a five table tournament with $4K up for grabs, there is a guy I have never met making crazy bets and somehow bringing it home by the river. I watch as he does this again and again. I am getting cards, but I am not getting flops to match them.

The Poker Gods are not smiling on me and all I am playing is a game called FOLD. I am picking up the odd pot by reading opponents and keeping my table image as that of a solid player. Who knows, I may have even been ahead when I raised the flop with nothing! The thing is, I am still in the game at the Final Table - and I am sitting opposite the Luck Bot who is sitting there, grinning broadly with a HUGE pile of chips.

Someone laughs and makes the comment that all we will be doing is deciding who comes second. The Luck Bot has more chips than all the other players combined. My immediate comment is that the huge chip stack coming to the Final Table is rarely the one that wins it. And it seems I was about to be proven right. FINALLY, the tide starts to turn - I start to get cards that hold up! From being the lowest stack I work up to being a middle stack. People are now dropping out and giving me their chips. Before too long there are three players left!

The important part of this story is that the whole time I am paying attention to the lucky guy - It seemed to me that the Luck Bots luck has finally run dry. He had not shown winning cards for more than thirty hands. Then I get that magic AA - We are three up and I am in the dealer position, so I have to act first against the blinds. Pocket Aces sounds fabulous, and it is - but in a position where you have to act first the only thought in my mind is, *"How do I get value here?"*

Right then, before the hand starts with the betting, the third player suggests a three-way split, based on chip stacks. The lucky guy just laughs, he figures he has the $4k in the bag. He still has more chips than the both of us combined. Arrogance is a wonderful thing to watch on a poker table, because it invariably hides fear. The game can turn on a dime and NO player on a final table can survive three big beats and be in good shape. More importantly, if someone is thinking they have it in the bag, they get careless.

That laugh told me he felt supremely confident. It meant he would call ANY small raise. I reinforce his belief by commenting, "I don't think we are in a position to negotiate here." Let's face it - I am holding Pocket Rockets - why would I want to negotiate?

Pause, breathe, think. Always stop before you act with a big hand. Try and get a read, look at the player you *want* to call in the eye and place your bet as a question. I just double the 14K blind and ask, very politely, "Twenty Eight?"

Let me never underestimate the power of asking a question when you make a bet - because making a bet IS asking a question. It is powerful because it opposes how most people believe you should bet. People think that if you have big cards you should make a big statement - thump down the chips, be aggressive, make a STATEMENT.

But why would I want to scare anyone away? I ask nicely, looking him in the eye to see his response. He does not return the eye contact, he did not even look up, just reached for chips.

I smile inside. He did not HESITATE to throw it in - But he neither did he raise! Small pockets, he would have re-raised. I figure Ace Rag or two picture cards. This is part of the language of betting, which I will cover shortly. The Big Blind folds, which is surprising because the extra 14K I asked for represented Six to One odds. I would have called with 2 4.

The flop falls 2 A 4 - I look interested. Why? There is no point in hiding a massive hand with feigned disinterest - People find that more suspicious. He is in the small blind and first to act. He does a minimum raise. Ah, Ace Rag - dangerous. A 3 or A 5 can get a straight here. He may have jagged two pair - who knows. But he is looking confident and has no idea I have flopped trips. By just calling here, I am saying I have an Ace something or pockets above the middle card of the flop. If I do a small re-raise he will call, if I go all-in he will fold unless he already have a made hand. How do I find out?

This is one of the most difficult things to play - you KNOW that with 98% of players you come against that you are well ahead, but this sort of Luck Bot might just have called with 3 5 and I am massively behind. But this is theory, reality asks, *"What to do?"*

I do NOT want to advertize I am holding a monster. I want to look helpless and let his arrogance run the show, so I give a small shake to my head and just call. I want to look like a guy fishing for the card he needs and it is half true because inside I am praying that the Poker Gods are with me. This is all you can do - The guy smiles, he believes he is ahead now.

Let us stop here and look at how REAL poker is played. It is all about belief, courage and faith in the notion you are good, or that your bluff will be good. You will never win a tournament without this - but when you have the goods, you want to encourage confidence in your opponent. This is how you get massive chip-ups. However you instil a false confidence in another does not matter - But be humble. If you want to set someone up for a fall, this is the best way to do it.

My luck bot is almost smirking, he feels so certain he has this in the bag. I am not doing this, his own arrogance has fuelled him. The voices in his head are saying he has this won. He is feeling supremely confident and THEN the next card comes - and he *lights up.*

The Turn is a FIVE - Which begs a question: D*id this fill out a straight for him?* He is first to act and once more bets the minimum. A Min Bet in this position is shouting that this five really suited him. He wants me to stay - he wants me to call. He has either filled a straight, or jagged two pair. I look at the 14K in chips he puts out and in response I repeat my original pre-flop question - *"Twenty Eight?"* I ask.

Once again: It is EXTREMELY important to make a bet look like a question. Why? It looks like I am not betting, just asking him how strong he is. And I am - his response will tell me. If he just doubles my re-raise I can be pretty certain he has the goods - I will be calling but will consider that I am behind and am drawing to a paired board to win. If he just calls he is not confidant. But If he PUSHES, he has two pair and thinks he is good. Well, my Luck Bot PUSHES, "All in!" he exclaims, staring hard at me for the first time in that hand.

I guess I could not suppress my smile and at that moment the look on his face went from supreme confidence to serious doubt.

Let's recap the obvious: All in bets when the next card can put you out of the game are not a bet, not a question, they are a gamble. There was *no hand* he could hold that could not be beaten by the river.

My read here is that he THINKS he is ahead, but now wants me out of the hand. Now, let me stress, the bet was a pointless overreach. He had three times my chip stack. If he HAD a straight, he would double my raise, or maybe triple. Either way, I would be crippled to call. I would have had to push back myself or fold. His 'all in' at that point is what convinced me he didn't have it. I call, he slams over A 5.

I turn an Ace. He smiles like a triumphant gladiator - Then he sees my OTHER Ace - His jaw drops, his eyes pop out of his head. I had waited an entire tournament, folding, folding, folding and folding again to his raising. The river was a nothing. The dealer, bless his Soul, commented with a wry grin on his face, *"Welcome to the new chip leader."*

The third player was gone by the next hand, giving his chips to the Luck Bot, who now wanted to do a deal. Now, you might think, "Why should I do a deal? I am the chip leader!" Here we come to a second principle of Poker, not playing against luck is one thing, but it is also wise to never trust luck. I agree to play the heads-up out on the basis of second going from $2K to $2500 and First going down to $3500.

WHY? You may believe I am hedging my bets, and I am, but it is more than this - By agreeing to play out to a more even split, the lower chip stack invariably becomes reckless. As soon as the deal is struck, he pushes with Q J. I have A K - I call. He misses and I take the money.

Only the Size of the Pot Matters

There is a VASTLY more important principle behind this story. Only the Size of the Pot Matters. To put this in perspective: *I won the tournament yet won less than ten percent of the hands of the guy who came second.* The MOST IMPORTANT RULE in POKER: ***It is not the NUMBER of hands you win, but the size of the pots.***

The principle is very simple: The size of the pot versus risk is the greatest determining factor in any decision you have to make in Texas Holdem. To win a hundred pots to make 100K in chips means one hundred risks you have to take. If you can win 100K chips in FIVE hands, this is significantly less risk and massively higher reward.

It is just Math, people. Very basic arithmetic.

How to Play the Lucky Player

However, let's put ourselves in the position of ending up in a hand against a lucky player - there is a way to play them. This is *not* the "Kill Phil" method of just pushing all-in pre-flop. Unless you have pockets do not even consider an 'all in' against a lucky player. Why? They will generally call your pre-flop all-ins because they have the chips to do so and they have been lucky while you have not.

What to do? You have to paint a picture that convinces them to fold, or you have to fold. This means a substantial raise pre-flop - set up the image you have Aces or Kings - then if the Flop shows no connected cards, no flush drawn, and if the Luck Bot is not smiling, a push AFTER the flop will usually get them out of the hand.

You do this for a number of reasons.

- One: you condition a player to how you 'play'
- Two: You are setting the scene for a big kill later on.

I played this "push on the flop" gambit three times with the Luck Bot before getting to the final table. It kept me in the game, but it also set him up for the one hand that mattered. THIS is why he called my small raise pre-flop with the hand where I held Aces. When I hit the trip Aces and DIDN'T push on the flop, he believed I was not strong. In his mind he had a read on how I played - Ergo: If I was ahead, I would push. But when he did a small raise on the flop and I did not push back with an 'All In', he read me as behind or on a draw. On the turn - where he now felt supremely confident - he raises and I only min-raise him. Again he reads this as weakness against his hand. Why? Because I had conditioned him as to 'how' I played. He then handed me all his chips in a hand where his absolute best outcome by the river was a split.

Let me be clear, it was *not* brilliant play that gave me the tournament. It was SURVIVING to get the sheer dumb luck of holding the right hand with the right opponent at the right time. Playing well ONLY determines you stay alive till your luck strikes!

Again: The money you pick up is NOT determined by how many times you win a hand, but by how *much you win* with the hands you play. Nothing else matters. Winning big pots when you are called means you HAVE to have the cards. In the meantime, it is all about lying, cheating, stealing, and just surviving till your luck finds you.

The Many Sides of Luck

There are many sides to luck, not just good luck or bad luck. There's a very different sort of luck, which has nothing to do with the cards you hold - It is the types of people you face. You may have a mouse on your table - any raise where he is not absolutely confidant causes him to fold. You don't need cards when you are heads up with this type. Then there is the pot-buyer - you may not think of them as luck, but let them raise a few hands, call if you have cards you like and, regardless if you hit or otherwise - when he raises the flop, push. They fold unless they have AA or have hit the top card.

The trick is RECOGNIZING Luck, in the many forms it can take. Most especially, bad luck. There are periods where nothing will run for you and nothing will change this. You can cajole, bluff and pretend you have the nutz only so far - eventually you will be called and without cards you will walk. Patience and timing win more than luck: *The hardest thing to do at a poker table is NOTHING.* But better doing nothing than being in low value pots or losing chips.

Cycles of the Moon

I think of it like the cycles of the moon - In the DARK of the moon, you can't see anything. You are stumbling around blind - In poker you are hoping to hit a Flop. As the moon grows, you start to get a bearing on where you are. But only with the full moon do you have good vision of what is around you. Clarity is everything in Poker.

The Dark of the Moon in Poker is difficult - You are in your personal "cloud" - a thing that stops you getting a clear read. It is the general downturn of luck and energy that put you off your game and it is always a fail to try and do anything in this sort of head space. The cycle WILL end, but here's the secret: *We will stay in this black cloud while we refuse to accept that other people have luck on their side.*

You cannot demand luck. You cannot bribe it, coerce it, of cajole it. You CAN change your attitude, however, and slowly Luck will return. It has always been there, it is just that we fail to see opportunity and capitalize on it when we are in a funk.

Hey Hey! You You! Get out of your cloud!

Have some patience, the tide will turn. In the meantime, avoid playing marginal cards and absolutely do NOT go "all In" when you are in the dark space. As you start to come out of it, you have a vision of a bit of good fortune - DO NOT ACT. Wait a little longer. When clarity arrives, you know it. You just see things better, judge things better and call and fold at the right time. This is the Full Moon and when you DO get this tide running, it is very hard to beat you.

You might call it luck, I call it timing.

I have watched many players over many years and the best ALWAYS get a sense when they are good - no matter the cards they hold. I watched one friend call an 'all in' coming up to the final on a major tournament - Before you say this is nothing - My friend called with Q 2 Spades. He ran out two pair on the flop (against an Ace that hit) and a flush by the river. The guy who pushed had AK.

How could he call? First, the player who pushed had been running badly - he looked unlucky. Two, my friend liked his cards. Three, he was not out to call. But most importantly - blinds were 30K - 60K - The guy pushed with 180K. He was in the Big Blind, it was costing 120K to call for 270K in chips. Further, my friend guessed the guy had AK and even STATED this as he called, while turning over Q2. You think this is crazy? Most do, but any two cards that are different represent 40% heads up. Seems crazy against AK but all Q2 has to do is hit a TWO and it wins.

My friend was in that bright space of clarity. No fear, no anger, nothing but the odds, the cards and the players. This is a truly beautiful place, the heaven of the Poker Gods. Heads up, any two cards and he correctly figured he only had to hit one of them. My friend went on to win that $70K tournament. A lot of money to risk with Q 2!

Find your HUM. Know your Odds. Find that space where you feel the cards, the table and the sense of when to call or fold. And ignore the whispers of the doubters all around you - And always remember, if other players hate you, you are playing well.

Luck is an Executioner, not a Judge.

Luck will not judge you. It runs WITH you or AGAINST you and it will either lift you on high, or throw you onto the dung heap. Luck is impersonal, uncaring and devoid of anything bar the moment. It is an unfaithful mistress. You can never trust luck, you can not believe in it, you cannot hope it will come along with you - but you CAN expect it to occur at some point. The trick is in guessing where that point is.

The first way to achieve this is to *stop judging your cards*!

Do not be a "Cardist!" Just as you call people who judge others by their color racist, people who judge cards by their numbers are Cardists.

It's truly incredible the number of times I have seen a player scoff at what someone has called with, yet those so-called crap cards goes on to beat their Aces. They bitch and moan and call the person a Donkey. Yet so often, only hands prior to this bad beat that same player will have played 'worse' cards and bad beat someone else. The two-faced nature of some people is very much like some of the cards they play!

The saying is: *Any Two Cards.*

If you wish to attract luck, you have to be non-judgemental, and generous. You have to call with marginal hands when pots odds say to call. You then fold gracefully if the Flop is poor for you and raise quietly when it comes up shining. Do not judge your cards as good or bad and only determine your course AFTER the flop. As a simple example: I have won far more hands with 5 3 suited than I have with K J.

Here's a secret: *People who judge their cards rarely take down large tournaments.* Why? A number of reasons, but primarily people KNOW when they have a Cardist at the table and will specifically play their rubbish knowing that the person most likely has AK or AQ.

You think that is crazy? What do you do when there are all low cards on the flop and you have AK? Simple - you do a follow-on raise. But if you get re-popped, THEN what do you do? You have three options, call, raise or fold - But the fact is, you haven't hit and your opponent could have anything. More importantly, when you KNOW the person you are against plays random cards, you are far more likely to fold.

Alternatively, there are many players who will push all in on the flop with their AK, regardless of what it is. If you KNOW the type of player they are, if you KNOW they only play high cards or pockets, you are at an ENORMOUS advantage. I have seen many an 'all in' called with a person holding K2 (or similar) when just the two hit - and the mighty AK their opponent held has died horribly.

Perception Opens Doors - Judgement Shuts Them

You create opportunity by knowing your opponent and how they will bet. When someone is a Cardist and is raising, they have pockets or high cards, so knowing this you have an impossibly great leverage over them. If all low cards hit, you can raise and they often will fold. If all high cards arrive, you can bow out without any sense of regret.

The flip side of the Cardist is the 'favorite' cards syndrome. Some people like J 7 and will call any raise with them. Others think 6 3 are the go. These players are difficult, because they BELIEVE in their cards - the belief is what makes the cards lucky for them - Yet point out the obvious and they fail to recognize it, that they are like so many gamblers who forget all the times they lost.

My favorite cards are, not surprisingly, AA followed by KK, after which I don't mind QQ. I like AK, I like ALL pockets. So tell me, WHY on earth would I chose 9 7 as my favorite cards? This sort of thinking is just stupid. The saying is, *"The race does not always go to the swift, nor the battle to the strong, but it is far better to bet that way."*

I win many hands with suited-connected cards, or similar, but the TOURNAMENT winning ones are the big pockets and AK. They are also the tournament losing ones.

What I want you to do is change your perception - Forget the notion of good versus bad cards. Stop imagining you have to have 'good' cards to win - What you need is CLEAR PERCEPTION. HOW you see things will determine how much you win, not the cards you hold. When you see clearly, you act confidently, and this CONFIDENCE is what creates your luck. How so? Confidence creates the image in people's heads that you are ahead - so they fold. CONFIDENCE CREATES LUCK!

LUCK IS NOT GETTING AA! With real poker players, the core of what people call Luck is a synthesis of observation and timing - They SEEM lucky, but the truth is they keep a clear head and get the read right.

So, on the flip side, is there any specific thing that ruins luck? Yes - Impatience. So many times I am watching the stack go down on a final table and all I am doing is folding blinds. You get to five blinds left and you feel you HAVE to act, so you push with the first decent hand.

Everyone understands this, but can you wait one more hand? I won a State title by waiting one more hand. I had only played four full hands to the river the entire day. Yes, I looked at a few dozen flops, bought the odd one to survive, but I really had been running dry.

I got down to ONE blind and look down - I have K5 under the gun. I am being forced to play, because I might get nothing next hand. I was about to push when I saw a player to my left look at his cards and instinctively go for his chips. This is almost ALWAYS a sign of a big hand. I fold. A good thing because he had pockets. The NEXT hand, I get QQ in the big blind - Talk about luck!

But the QQ was not the 'real' luck - Five people came into this hand - That is 600K in chips at the 100K blind. But even THIS is not the real luck - My amazing luck was the drunk guy beside me who pushed 'all in' on the flop, isolating everyone out of the hand. I am now heads up! Everyone else folds and he flips over J6, laughing, calling the other players weak. He had nothing - QQ holds and final table is called three hands later.

I had waited all day and now my luck starts to run. But it was more than just luck, I felt clarity and focus - My read on what people held along with my feel for the cards was in good form. I was able to read the players, the deck,

Big Blind, I look down and see my luck turn!

everything. This can happen - a thing the Tibetans call "Vidya" or "True Seeing". When THIS strikes you become unbeatable.

If only I could give a prescription on how to create it! It is a combination of grind, trust in the Poker Gods, and down-home common sense mixed with a whole lot of patience. I won that tournament.

As a funny side bar the same drunk guy was heads-up with me for the prize. Only then did he notice all my chips and his jaw hit the ground, "Where did you get THOSE from?" he asked.

"You," I said. "Because of your stupid betting just before the final table, you kept me in the game." He just looked confused, then went All In on every hand. I could see he was rattled, so waited. I get pocket fives and just pay the blind. Most would push, considering that just calling a very unwise course - but I knew he would do the pushing for me. He does! I call. He turns over 2 3 - I turn the 55 - he seems unfazed "I know I am good," he says, "I can see the 2 3 on the flop already!"

He got them! 2 3 arrives! Then a 5 falls. He cheered, not seeing what I held. The dealer looked puzzled. "Two pair!" he shouts.

The dealer explained, "You have two pair against trips, Sir."

He is 'still' full of beans, "Come on, give me a Two or a Three!" he shouts as the Turn is, appropriately, turned.

"It won't help you, Sir," the dealer explained. "Any Two or Three and your opponent will have the better full house. You need two 2's or two 3's to win."

He didn't get them - I still laugh at his indomitable and extremely drunk sense of being unbeatable, no matter the cards. It got him to second place - But to get number one you have to possess TWO important criteria: Despite what people say, you have the CARDS that win an all in and you have to MAKE Luck. Cards are self-evident, you think? Not at all. Making luck and getting winning cards are two completely different animals. Making Luck is all about spotting Opportunity and making THAT work for you.

Now we come to the most important part of the book! How to create your Luck by building your opportunities.

'Luck Is What Happens When Preparation Meets Opportunity'
Seneca

CREATING OPPORTUNITY

"Last night I stayed up late playing poker with Tarot cards.
I got a full house and four people died."
Steven Wright

Let's look at how we MAKE luck. This requires a subtle combination of table presence and raising at the correct time. This is not only getting a read on your opponents, it is cultivating a presence so that THEY believe they have a read on you.

If opportunity doesn't knock, build a door.

Milton Berle

We all call for Luck, but really, if you are constantly showing your opponent your cards by the river, you are not really playing poker - you are playing luck. No, you want to create OPPORTUNITY - which is as much capitalizing on the opponents weakness as it is bluffing at the right time. Spotting your Opportunity is where you MAKE Luck.

So how do we create Opportunity and how do we capitalize on it?

The first basic principle of generating Opportunity is appearing to be predictable while you are being random. You want people to put you as a certain 'type' of player, whatever that might be. As an example: If you appear to be the 'Rock'- The guy who only raises when he has a hand' - and you make a bet with 2 / 3 in your hand, observant players will fold unless they have premium cards. If you have a table image of being someone who constantly raises (Not a bad image to have!) then they will call you when you have Aces and have hit the flop big time.

You make create Opportunity PRIMARILY by creating an appearance!

After the table image is set, you play each specific type of player in such a way so as to construct *in their minds* a belief of what you hold. This is a refined art and not something a book can teach you. But I will outline the basic strategies. Primarily, you need to be able to correctly pick the type of player you are against and play your cards accordingly.

Playing the Cherry Bomber: We start with this lot because there is no effective strategy against Cherry Bombers. They are irrational players. You have to trap play them, but in a specific way - The most effective gambit is to insult them on a continual basis till they hate you. Position is everything against Cherry Bombers - Wait until they are in a hand and doing stupid raises AND you flop a monster. Just call them names that are permissible at the table - use intellect as your weapon - and when you have Aces DO NOT raise, just call them names. They will get so annoyed they will just go All In on any draw.

Playing the Big Man: They need to look big, so fuel their sense of importance when you want them to fold, deride it when you want them to call. This type raises with small pockets or two high cards. Your opportunity arises with this player primarily when you have hit something, anything, and they call you to the River with their AK. If you want them OUT of the hand, tell them that you respect their play, and that they are a staunch, solid performer. It is only because you really don't want them catching their card that you are going 'All In'.

Playing the Donkey: You have to be careful, what you see as a created opportunity to collect chips they may see as a perfect opportunity to gamble. It pays to talk Donkeys through a hand - they are not used to this. Ask them if they really believe their cards are lucky. Point blank simple questions cut through the fog that is their mind. Things like, *"I know I am well ahead, but I also know no cards are safe, so I am going to make a very large raise, one that will cost you the tournament if you don't get what you need, OK?"* You watch them fold.

Playing the Pot Buyer: Cultivate a sense they are the boss. Just call pre-flop and fold to any raise post-flop. Do a few times, then re-raise their post-flop raise. Unless they hit a monster, they will rarely raise your raise. You then have to do a large raise on the turn to get them to fold. If they have nothing they generally will give up because you have set up the belief by all your folds that you MUST have a monster. The point is NOT the cards you hold or the chips in play, but setting the player up to believe they know HOW you play. By the same token, if you jag two pair or better and they have hit the top card, the pot-buyer will call ANY raise and they will give you ALL their chips.

Playing the Old Woman: If you have hit - Small Ball is the game. This is the art of making small, incessant raises when they are in a hand. If they just call they have an ace or pockets, or have hit. If they have pockets over the flop, they will push. You won't get them off any hand where they think they are good, so you have to make them think they are not. A large raise on the river WILL be called, but an All In on the turn generally won't. Play them according to the cards that fall. Outrageous bluffs usually work, unless they hit their Ace. Keep doing it till they get angry and call you with anything . You drive these players till they run out of patience, then they make mistakes.

Playing the Chaser: This is fairly straightforward but risky. If you feel you are good on the flop, three bet the blind. If there is no straight or flush possibility on the turn, push all in. But be warned: I have seen Chasers call an 'All In' even when a player accidentally exposed their twp pair. On one occasion, two players forgot the Chaser was in the hand, the first pushed, the other called, they turn over two pair and trips. The Chaser can win with a straight IF a ten falls. It is the ONLY card that can save him - and yet he STILL CALLED, and he GOT!
There is nothing you can do to defend against sheer dumb luck. Playing the chaser is really a game of odds - The basic rule is, if you want them out of a hand, commit as much as you can afford on the TURN, not on the flop or river.

Playing against Trap Players: These are the hardest to negotiate, especially as the most proficient will not be passive and commit to small bets and small re-raises at apparently random times. Because they fold so much, if they are calling, you have to put them on a big hand. A little secret, two pair is rarely good enough when a good trap player is staying in a hand. You have to play the slow game with this type, nibble until they lose patience. This is the dividing line - No one is immune to the vagaries of fate and after too many folds, the trap player will often call a push with QJ or similar. You have to smell when they are worn down and THEN push. Otherwise, you play your cards till you have hit trips, etc. and hope they have something solid to call you with.

Playing the Professional: Despite what you might think, these are the easiest ones to set up. Why? Because they tend to be arrogant. Plus, they tend to play cash games more than tournaments, and chips have entirely different values in a tournament game. The professional will have a variety of gambits, but overall they play to weakness - So trap play them, act weak. Then, as soon as you sniff you are ahead, massively re-raise their bet. A professional will ALWAYS fold if they think they are behind - But a warning, they will NEVER fold AK or similar if you don't have enough chips to threaten their stack.

Playing the Unreadable: There is also the unknown player - the one you haven't been able to catagorize. It is often someone affected by drugs or booze, or both! Medical pills mixed with a little booze can turn a nice little lady into a crazy Amazon. These are ALWAYS your greatest risk. There is no way to play these other than fold till you have a hand, and then push back hard against any raise they make. I give an example to illustrate this following the Summary.

SUMMARY: In ALL these cases, you are winning hands by knowing the type of player you are up against, and creating OPPORTUNITY by playing to their weakness. You LOOK as if you are running Lucky, which creates an aura where you can control the table far more easily. Luck builds on Luck, but it starts with you creating the opportunity!

Playing the Unreadable - Example

It is always tricky when a new player you don't know comes to a table. In this case there was a woman, we will call her Betty, I had never met on this table where I wake up with a monster. She was well dressed, polite, demure. She seemed a very careful player and I am already placing her in the Old Woman zone. I am in the middle position and I have J J. The new player just calls, so I bet HARD - ten times the blinds. Why? Next to act on my left is a KNOWN Old Woman. What is more, I can see she is liking her cards. We will call her Anne.

If Anne hits she will call any raise. If she has an Ace, she will call a significant raise regardless of the flop of the value of the pot - I know this, she is the absolute classic "Old Woman" player - literally.

In this hand, Anne calls without hesitation. Unfortunately, so does Betty, the other unknown player. My TEN TIMES the blind raise got me TWO callers - I only wanted one - As I say, I don't know Betty but she seems to be a safety player and otherwise pretty clueless. In fact, she appears genuinely confused by the ten times the blind action - But she calls anyway.

The flop comes down Ten High with two low cards, one is a diamond - I can see Anne already reaching for chips - I know she has a ten, most likely Ace Ten. I also know she will call ANY raise - So, as first to act, I push 'All In' - I want to make it look as if I am trying to buy the pot. Anne does not hesitate - she snap calls with what is close to her entire stack.

Betty, however, flitters about and does not appear to even be able to count her chips. I have no idea what she has,but she must be on a draw. She tries to make the call with less than ten percent of the raise. the dealer says she has placed insufficient chips in the pot to call.

She dithers about in confusion - It was a pot that consumed most everyone's chips, so it was 'All In' or nothing at this point. After several minutes - when she realizes she can't take the chips back - Betty decides to just call - The betting is still live and the next card is a diamond, the second diamond. Anne Checks. Betty raises the minimum. Anne calls.

Then, another diamond, both girls check - I flip over JJ. Anne flips A 10 - while Betty flips over AQ Diamonds - she didn't even bet her nut flush on the river! I just shake my head and walk away - Making Luck - I made some luck, alright - I made luck for Betty.

In 99% of the circumstances there is no way a person with two random overs will call an all in like that on the flop. There was no way anyone at the table had the odds to call, even with Anne hitting the ten with her A 10 - I got the player I WANTED in the hand and another I didn't - I should have tripled up but instead I was walking to the car.

There are no end to bad beat stories and there is a reason for this - Not just LUCK - I committed my stack in a hand where I did not know the type of player I was with. When she was dithering, if I had known her type, I could have talked her down and she would have folded.

I could have said, "I know you WANT to call, but you must know one of us is well ahead. Unless you have Aces, with respect, you really should fold and not risk your Tournament on a draw."

But to be fair, who would have possibly imagined you could meet an Old Woman, Cherry Bomber, Trap Player, Chaser, Newbie Novice all wrapped up in one player? I never knew it was possible until that hand!

You cannot beat luck, but you CAN negotiate around it. You can know your players by watching how they act, how they bet, and when they fold. Look closely for the small signals, the tells that speak if they have a big hand or a hope. Betting is the language of the poker player, working opportunity is the real leverage they hold, not their cards. Knowing the type of players you have at the table means you CAN bet in such a way as to increase your odds, improve your luck, and lessen your risks. Yet to do this effectively, you have to understand the types of odds at play in any given hand.

ODDS and EVENS

Here we will discuss the various types of odds, and what evens them out.

"In the long run there's no luck in poker,
but the short run is longer than most people know."
Rick Bennet

Here we will be looking at Long Odds, (Outs) Implied Odds and Short Odds. This is a very short summary of the basic calculations that make up the Math of Poker. You do NOT have to be a mathematician to work these out - they are very simple.

But to keep thing really easy - any single card that you need roughly counts for two percent. If you need a four and there are no fours to be seen, then with four fours in the deck you have 4 x 2% = 8% - every card to come gives you an eight percent chance of hitting a Four.

When we think of ODDS, most people look at percentages. When we think of percentages we tend to be looking at a thing called "Outs". To be clear, let me define an OUT for you: An **OUT is something you DO NOT HAVE but HOPE TO GET.** In a nutshell, an "out" is a card you need that gets you "out" of the hole you are in. Always remember: An "Out" is a card you DO NOT HAVE, but need if you are to win.

It may seem strange that so many people base their percentages on something they do not have and hope to get, but this is how modern poker is played. Here we will go past the science of Outs and look at a wider range of considerations, but the sum total of everything we are looking at is finding a way to determine the VALUE of a hand BEFORE we bet into it or call a raise.

The calculation of your chances in any hand is like shopping for a new car. The salesman says, "This is worth $10K !" But you look and see areas that say otherwise. You point out some rust, a knock in the motor. You decided it is not worth the asking price and walk.

OR you notice the high performance motor fitted, the high spec shock absorbers, a lot of hidden value that makes the $10K look cheap, so you buy in. It is the same with poker hands, someone makes a bid for the pot - This presents you with THREE OPTIONS:

- You see no value in it for yourself and fold.
- You see it could be valuable, and call.
- You see it is worth WAY more and re-raise

But HOW do you work out the inherent value in the cards before you? This is what odds are used for.

Real Life Example:

Let's take a look at a real life example. You hold Q J of Diamonds, the flop is A K diamonds, 9 clubs. You don't know it, but you are against K 9 and A J - and both are betting in. You have to call, there are so many OUTS, especially with the 2% call for the Ten of diamonds that gives you the ultimate hand, the Royal Flush.

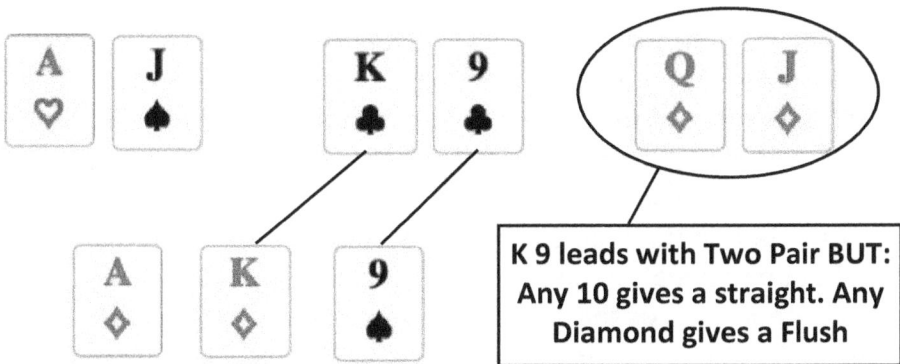

> K 9 leads with Two Pair BUT: Any 10 gives a straight. Any Diamond gives a Flush

Your "Outs" are any Ten, any Diamond, possibly QQ or JJ following. The diamonds or the ten are the only ones we seriously consider. There are NINE diamonds left, that's **nine outs**. There are FOUR tens left, but one of those is a diamond, so that is **three tens**. three plus nine = **Twelve OUTS**. At roughly two percent per card, you have twenty four percent per card flip with two cards to come - Twelve OUTS on the Turn and Twelve on the River - forty eight percent makes it a roughly 50/50 split with the random option of hitting double Q or Double J.

Extremely good odds to win the hand. But we always hear about Odds, what about the EVENS?

Whoever talks about the EVENS? There ARE other people in this hand and the cards THEY get are the EVENS that lessen your Odds. What Outs do THEY have that will IMPROVE their hand? These cards EVEN your odds. The next card is a Jack - Giving AJ Two Pair. Hitting the Jack in this circumstance EVENS the odds against you. The cards THEY can get now work into the picture. Any Ace, Jack, King OR Nine gives one of your opponents a full house. These are the EVENS which weaken your OUTS.

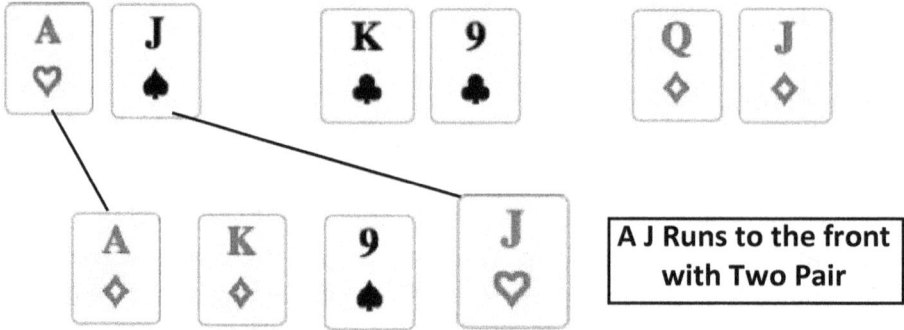

| A ♥ | J ♠ | | K ♣ | 9 ♣ | | Q ♦ | J ♦ |

| A ♦ | K ♦ | 9 ♠ | J ♥ | **A J Runs to the front with Two Pair** |

The basic argument for not getting into this area of EVENS is that they are impossible to calculate. This is very true - You cannot know what the other player is holding, but you CAN consider what they MIGHT be holding. in fact, if you don't you are destined to lose.

Let us look closely at this. You have looked down and seen what appears to be an absolute monster of a hand, one where you are willing to call ANY bet on the flop. The Turn is a JACK, which weakens your hand, but do you realize this? It doesn't matter - you still see any diamond or any Ten as the winning cards. A Nine of Diamonds kills you, however. What this means is A SMALL ADJUSTMENT AND that you still have a twenty two percent equity WITH your OUTS.

What does this situation add up to? It means you still have equity to call a raise, but how much? You presently have a better than one in five chance (20%) to win on the River. Logically, if the bet that follows the Turn means your call is less than 20% of the NET pot, you have what is called VALUE to call. OUTS are one thing - But VALUE is everything.

VALUE now comes into play. **What is your POT VALUE to call?**

This is when we take your OUTS and convert these into your POT ODDS. The POT ODDS are what makes something worth calling. The value of the incoming bets are weighed against the net value of the percentage you hold in OUTS.

Calculating POT VALUE

At this moment there is 8500 in the Pot. You can see the first to act reaching for chips - he bets the value of the pot - 8500 - you can see the other player already reaching for chips. With the 8500 in the pot from pre-flop betting, if the other person calls, as you know they will, and YOU call, you then have 34000 to play for. { (3 x 8500) + Pot of 8500 = 34000. } What is your POT VALUE in this scenario?

Look at the NET POT. Your 8500 CALL equals one quarter of 34000 - so if everyone calls, your COST is twenty five percent of the Pot against the twenty two percent equity you hold.

**8500 POT +
3 X 8500 call =
34000 net pot**

Your Call = 25% of this Pot.

**Your OUTS say
CALL EQUITY is 22%**

You are DOWN 3%

You are down 3% -Would you fold? You might think about it - but is there a cash bonus for a royal flush? If there is, you have to add THAT into the mix of what constitutes value. However, let's face it, the lure of a Royal Routine is staring you in the face and no one is going to fold this. So you are now hoping and wishing for the diamond or a ten .

What to do? Next, you take a walk down logic lane - Your NEXT step is to look at the cost to your stack should you lose. This equals your POSITION should you lose and it must be part of your calculations.

OVERVIEW: You have 30K in chips. You are left with 21500 if you miss. This is a playable stack - you are not crippled.

Now you balance your calling value against your risk to reward - WIN and you will hold over 53K in chips. This almost doubles your stack and a miss is not putting you out of the game.

The Math adds up: You are GOING to call this! The ONLY reason you wouldn't has nothing to do with odds and everything to do with whether you are feeling lucky or otherwise. You would have to be feeling very unlucky not to call.

Only Consider POT VALUE with a CALL on the FLOP

If we ignore OUTS, ignore ODDS, and consider nothing but the VALUE of the POT you see that for another 8500K you have the chance to almost DOUBLE UP your stack. These figures say you have to call, despite the fact that the POT VALUE says you are sitting at three percent against calling.

No one is folding this. And there are more esoteric reason why you won't. Just the added playing power you can achieve is worth the risk. Poker is not about just winning a hand, it is about getting to a place of power, and only CHIPS and TABLE PRESENCE give you this. And without chips, your Table Presence isn't worth a damn!

A positive outcome puts you in a position to play more hands, look for opportunity, test the waters, and get chips. So - This is also part of the VALUE of this pot you are bidding for. Therefore: the VALUE of the Pot to your *overall game* in these scenarios is another DETERMINING FACTOR you should consider.

Yet, this is what your MIND tells you to do - what does your HEART say? Your final decision has to come from instinct, yet here there is one certainty - the bait of the royal hits your greed button and all refined senses are tossed out the window. You are going to call - No one would fold in this situation.

Play to Generate Opportunity. Chips give you the POWER to do this.

Pot Value is all about what it is worth NOW, and what the consequences are NEXT - *Calculating this forces you to stop and think.* When you do the math the effect is that you get to cool down. When you stop thinking that potential Royal in front of you, you start to see the obvious. Logic says that two players coming in hot means you are likely behind by the turn, yet now you know you are behind. You are ahead in this respect. The other players do NOT know if they are ahead or behind. At least you KNOW you need a Ten or a Diamond.

Based on ALL of the above, my action when it comes to the 8500 raise by A J would ONLY be a choice whether I should Call or PUSH.

Can I bluff by representing a straight? Do I smile, thank them for the chips, and go 'All In'? It depends on my Position - This is my position on the table PLUS the position in the overall game. Here I have to tell you, if it were not the fact that this was the first damn hand I played in that tournament I would have gone 'All In' and prayed for them to fold. This is a true story - in real life I just called. Truth to tell, I wasn't feeling lucky but at the same time, I had to see that river.

So, you ask - Did I get my 640,000 to 1 Royal? No - I missed. This exercise is to point out the process by which you come to decisions. You NEVER trust to luck. You ALWAYS count your Pot Size and thus resolve your Pot Value, PLUS you consider the position you hold if it all goes South OR North - this represents your true picture.

The Message: There are many factors that get rolled up into any single decision. These things form up what we call your IMPLIED ODDS. Your Implied Odds are what the overall factors add up to, and these change according to your position on a table of in a tournament. Early hands in a tournament offer you very different choices to mid-game play or towards final table gambits.

IMPLIED ODDS

This brings us to a very tricky subject, one rarely spoken of. This is the little known and less understood factor that determines the course of betting, your IMPLIED ODDS. This is the collected wisdom, if you will, or calling, raising or folding in any given hand. It is like getting a mile above yourself and looking down - It is the gestalt of your whole game.

In any given hand, you are either calling to value, calling to outs, or you are raising because you want people out of the Pot or you are cultivating a table presence. All these factors set up your overall game at the table you are on. ALL of this is IMMEDIATE. It is RIGHT NOW and ALL THIS rolls into what we call our IMPLIED ODDS.

Below is the situation. What do we DO with this? We need to use this to work the table and build our presence.

| A ♡ | J ♠ | | K ♣ | 9 ♣ | | Q ♢ | J ♢ |

You Hold Q J with a 22% Call Equity in a 8500 Pot

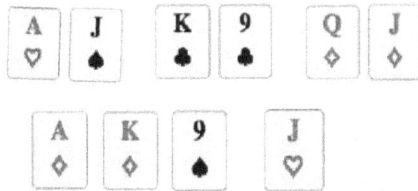

| A ♢ | K ♢ | 9 ♠ | J ♡ |

OUTS	Any Diamond bar the Nine - Any Ten (9 - 1) + 3 = 11 - Equity of 22%
+	
POT VALUE	RAISE of 8500 on TURN. Three callers plus the pot = 34000 chips Your call of 8500 = POT VALUE of 25%
+	
NET RISK	Loss of 8500 Call leaves you with 21500
+	
NET GAIN	Net Win gives you 53000
=	**Loss does not cripple your stack. Win puts you in a position to control the table.**

You are rolling everything into a decision to act. Let's look at scenarios that are offered with different bets, and see how it affects the decisions to call, raise, or fold.

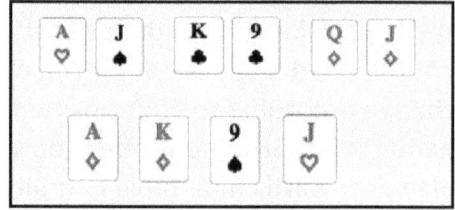

Let's suppose that the TURN bet was only 2000, not 8500. I am in the middle position - What to do?

Well, first I do a whole lot of thinking, considering and weighing of options. The different size bet changes the whole way of dealing with this. In this instance, it is a *given* I will CALL, the real question is should I RAISE, and if I raise, HOW MUCH? The POT ODDS and VALUE are there, but my next action needs to consider not just this hand, but how I am setting up the table. You are not just playing for THIS hand - Everyone on the table is watching, seeing what I do and how I bet.

8500 POT +
3 X 2000 call =
14500 net pot

Your Call = 13.8%
of this Pot.

Your OUTS say
CALL EQUITY is 22%

You are UP 8%

ASK QUESTIONS - MAKE A STORY out of the SITUATION

Who is there? What types of players are looking at my actions and deciding what sort of player "I" am? If I have a Pot Buyer and I just call, it will encourage him to raise me in other hands. If I have an Old Lady, they won't pay any attention to what I do unless I push all in. You are not just working out your odds in THIS hand, you are also calculating your chances of getting chips from people in OTHER hands. The CALLING or RAISING OPTIONS that are IMPLIED is a fairly esoteric combination of many factors, but when you see Poker Champions making the most unlikely calls and raises, and winning - THIS is what they are relying on.

THIS is the SCIENCE of Poker and the only thing that beats Luck.

The question here is HOW do I work this situation, in order to CREATE OPPORTUNITY, both NOW and in OTHER HANDS. I don't just call, I don't just raise - I make a small spectacle of the situation. I might make a comment, like, "Too Cheap!" and re-raise. I might laugh and say, "I hope you got the straight, cause that two pair won't help you." I want to set a scene, paint a picture and put the fear of the Poker Gods into my opponents - ALL of them at that table. I want to IMPLY that I am way good and that THEY are the ones chasing to catch up.

SHORT ODDS

A ♡	J ♠	K ♣	9 ♣	Q ♦	J ♦

A ♦	K ♦	9 ♠	J ♡

However, table presence aside, let's keep running with this example. Before the Turn hits I am in a hand where I am drawing to any Diamond or any Ten. What I need to consider at this point are what my SHORT ODDS might be. With any Flush Draw you fall into the area of what we call SHORT ODDS, where I am looking at the IMMEDIATE chances of what might be the next card and what this will mean to my hand.

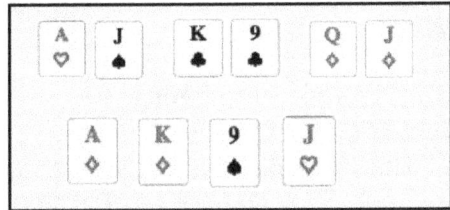

Short Odds are exactly this - SHORT. They are the odds of absolute certainties of what can occur on the very next card. These start AFTER the Flop - Short Odds are peculiar to games like Texas Hold-Em and only start when you have cards on the table. The ODDS of NOW, or Short Odds, describe what is a CERTAINTY on the next card.

Long Odds represent the game of OUTS, these are the averages that hold true over thousands of hands - but not necessarily THIS hand. The SHORT ODDS are the immediate NOW odds. This is specifically important with flush draws - because the cold hard fact is that the *next card* will be one of four suits AND one of thirteen cards. This is a CERTAINTY. Short Odds say one in four for a Diamond. I have twenty five percent for a flush whereas Long Odds say Nine out of Fifty Two cards, or roughly eighteen percent. A seven percent difference is THE WORLD. With two cards to come, this is a fourteen percent improvement, or a calling equity, using Long Odds, of having another SEVEN cards to help you win over the Turn and the River.

Next we look at getting a Ten. This means hitting one of thirteen cards - Long Odds say eight percent, Short Odds agree with this. One of these Tens is a Diamond and already been counted in the flush draw. Your SHORT ODDS are Twenty Five percent for a Diamond, plus Six Percent for a Ten. This adds to 31% per card as my SHORT ODDS. **This is 62% over Two Cards!** This represents a One in Three chance PER CARD.

SHORT ODDS

Next card can only be one of four suits = 25% short odds

Any 10 (less the diamond) = 6%

CALL EQUITY is now 31% or 9% HIGHER than with Long Odds

"Limit poker is a science, but no-limit is an art. In limit, you are shooting at a target. In no-limit, the target comes alive and shoots back at you." - **Jack Strauss**

Working the Bet

How does this change the betting scenario with the Flush draw?

The Jack falls and the first to act raises just 2K. Now there is 10500 in the pot I will obviously call 2000 - but I would not just call. I would TALK to my opponents with the language of betting!

My SHORT ODDS say I can call ONE THIRD of the chips on the table. 8500 + 2000 = 10500 in front of me, while my 2000 would make it 12500. You KNOW the next player will call, which will make it 14500.

Before I bet, I have to set the scene - I want to increase the value of the pot, but I ALSO want to test the third player. Why? I want to know how strong their resolve might be. I am calling to the pot value, PLUS I am trying to reduce risk by getting the third player to fold. And further, I am getting INFORMATION by how they react.

A small ongoing bet from the first player suggests he is either sitting with a made hand or controlling the betting and drawing to a better card. *I need to get more information.* There was 8500 in the pot, plus the Turn bet of 2000 - this equals 10500 in chips. Just calling this raise represents a twenty percent equity in the pot - cheap for the risk to reward. But just calling tells the other players my cards are only worth twenty percent. I don't want the other players thinking this!

So, I would three bet that raise, making it 6000 and lifting the pot to 16500. Remember - I am drawing to the absolute NUTZ - I have nothing to fear from the flush draw, while any diamond bar the Nine, or any ten means I am good. It is therefore IMPLIED that I lift the stakes. Plus I want to put the fear of the Poker Gods into the people who call. I have no idea what they hold, but the right raise at the right time paints a picture of CONFIDENCE. In their heads I am now pointing out how there is so much AGAINST the two pair they both currently hold.

The third player calls, as does the first. Neither pushes All In, which tells me a lot. If they had the straight they would have. So I have talked the talk, walked the walk, and set things up for the final card.

In chess, the luck is about three percent, while in poker it is 10 times more.
Ivo Donev: *(International Chess master - Pictured above)*

Position Position Position

This example was an actual hand that happened early in the tournament. If we were coming up to final table, where fear decides actions more than cards, I would have either pushed 'All In' or folded the Turn. Position, be it on the table, in the tournament, *or where you have situated yourself in the minds of your opponents,* is everything.

Building a position in the minds of those on your table is part of the your IMPLIED ODDS. These are the GESTALT - the Pot Value, the Betting, the Cards, the people in the hand, the people at the table AND your Position - This is ALL part of your calculations with your Implied Odds.

On any poker table, at all times, you are positioning yourself to CAPITALIZE on and CREATE OPPORTUNITY. Luck follows Opportunity. All of this is part and parcel of the ODDS you are working with.

If you can remember this simple guideline, it will make you a lot of chips. *When you are in position, bet.* There are many positions, however! It is a little bit like the Kama Sutra.

Let us look at the main positions you will encounter.

Last to Act: In any hand where you are the last person to act in any given round, it is generally wise to put out some sort of bet. It doesn't matter if you have anything, you want to see who folds.

Coming up to Break: It is amazing how many times a push as you come up to a break will only get you one caller, and it will always be the low chipped player who thinks "Chip up or chip out!". The Break is when they start asking if they want to keep grinding, or see if they get lucky.

Coming up to Final Table. People start to play extremely tight when the Final Table is only a player or two away. They don't want to be the one walking home this late into the tournament. Being aggressive in this position, IF you have a table presence, will earn you a LOT of chips.

Start of Tournament: People are wary about large bets and calling with marginal hands inside the first two blind levels of a big tournament. It is also a good time to get your table presence up and get a read from who is at your table. Pushing buttons works.

New to an Established Table: This is a great time to put in a large bid for a pot. People don't know you are are wary of calling a large raise.

Example of Playing Position

I was on a table where I was getting a lot of premium cards. I pretty much always raise with anything decent when I am in the dealer position and when no one else has raised. As it happened, of course, the same player was in the Big Blind every time I raised. He was convinced I was targeting him.

At one point, I get Kings and I am on the Dealer Button. No one has raised, I am certainly not going to let everyone into the hand, so I do a substantial raise - four times the blind. The Big Blind STAMPS his chips down to call. Everyone else folds. The flop runs out with A K K - It is checked down to me, a difficult spot to capitalize on.

I make a small bet, asking, "Does anyone have anything of this?"

The Big Blind is triumphant. He is absolutely certain I am buying the pot and he shoves, saying, "You have been pushing me off pots the WHOLE EVENING. Now let's see what you got - I am ALL IN!"

Obviously, I call - he flips over his triumphant Ace - Six. I flip over Quad Kings, and he is stunned. He almost starts apologising for his actions, and blubs, "Oh, I thought you had nothing. I was certain you had been bluffing the whole night." He was in shock. His entire image of me as the chip bully was shattered and he was walking home.

Thank the Poker Gods he bet the one time I DID have cards!

But more than this, if he truly thought he was ahead, why did he push? He could have three bet me and at least given me a bit of sport to play with. People who get angry on a poker table are boring - Yes, I was happy to have his chips, but the truth was, I had not given the guy two minutes thought up till that point.

If you are getting upset on a poker table, remember this important bit of information, "No one cares! They just want your chips."

The point is, position works. It is the most important part of poker and playing position well will give you the life sustaining chip ups that get you to the final table. And you can ALSO play the 'wrong' position well, and get people to fold. *This is the black art of poker*.

For Example: Under the Gun is a terrible place to raise, or so they say. But if you have respect at a table and you raise under the gun, people think you have a real monster. You use position as part of your paint kit to illustrate how you wish to be seen.

EXAMPLES:

What say we bounce some options about, to get the idea of how we might look at any given hand we have, and how we might play it.

Let's say I land an open-ended straight draw on the flop. I have 9 10 Clubs and the flop is 8 J 5. If a 7 or a Q turns up, I am good. There are thirteen cards in the deck and I need a 7 or Q - that is 2/13th of the deck, or 15.38%. ([100 divided by 13] x 2 = 15.38)

Needs 7 or Q to make a straight = 15.38% Calling Equity per card

Let's go back to the ROYAL FLUSH DRAW hand. Here we look at landing two pair versus drawing to the flush. Obviously, if the board pairs with one of their cards they fill a house and getting ANY flush, bar the Royal, puts my Q J in deep water. I am pretty sure that one of the other two players in this hand have hit two pair. What are my odds?

This is where their outs come into play. I need any diamond or any ten. K 9 needs another K or a 9. A J needs another A or a J. There are 2 x A, 2 x K, 2 x J, 2 x 9 left in the deck.

Now we come to the OTHER side of short odds. Collectively they have 8 outs, 8 chances from 52 cards that the NEXT card will give them a full house. Not individually, mind - collectively. Each player is calling for 4 cards, or 8%, to become bullet proof - but COLLECTIVELY I am up against 16% AGAINST me by the river. 32% - 16% = 16% - Even if I get my flush, my odds are HALVED and I am completely unaware of it.

My 32% Equity Dives to just 16% because of the COMBINED EVENS my opponents can get that kill my hand

The Seven Cards that Absolutely Kill Me: Any A K 9 or J

PROBABILITY

This sound scientific, yet also very uncertain. Probability is a study of random plausibility. For instance, what is the probability of a BLUE QUEEN turning up? Answer = Zero. This is a certainty, there are no Blue Queens in the deck. This might sound crazy, but knowing what CANNOT happen is as important as what can.

Fact: It is a CERTAINTY your opponents hold two cards - Fact: ALL players can make a hand on the Flop. FACT: No two players can have the same hand. It might seem obvious, and it is, but probability deals with the obvious and quantifies it.

Now, in Poker you SHIFT Probability with PERCEPTION. If you are a good reader of people on a poker table, you are shifting the odds tremendously in your favor. Someone is in the hand and betting big, is your read that they are idiots, or that they have something? If the latter, then the PROBABILITY of two pair or trips is high. Based on my READ, I calculate different odds. EG: Should the board pair, even if I catch a flush, I am at risk of walking into a full house.

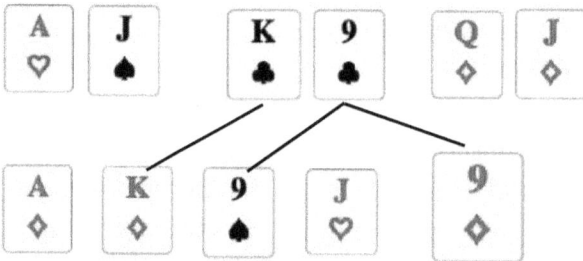

Your READ determines PROBABILITY and thus your choice of ACTION.

Q J has a FLUSH but what is the PROBABILITY someone filled a Full House?

Do you call their 'All In'??

Let's say the river is a 9 Diamonds. I have the flush, but what is my READ. I have already understood I may be against two pair at the Turn - Did they fill a house? What to do? This comes down to raw ability and the certainty of your read on the opponents. If someone raises they may earnestly believe they are good with a straight, or a lower flush, they may be bluffing and have nothing. HOW do I get a read?

Start talking. Look at the people in the hand, and ask questions. Ask, "How many of us got our boat on the river? Is mine better than yours, I just don't know." This sort of thing. It is called FISHING and a lot of tournaments say that unless you are heads up, you cannot talk about your hand with another player, so you don't talk to them - You ask other people on the table.

"Who do you think got the full house, and who thinks their flush is good?" That sort of thing. You air questions not for answers, you ask questions to get a reaction. A small clue: The person WITH the full house will almost never complain, they WANT you to raise. The person without it will be the one telling you to shut up.

You figure your chances of a person holding a Full House by talking and observing through the entire hand.

Choosing Your Course of Action

The Action in a game is what you DO. REACTING to what people do is a losing strategy. On a new table it is important that you stamp your presence as a player to be reckoned with. ACTING creates energy and CORRECT Action creates respect, but you can also be passively active. To whit: You might be calling just to fold to someone you know will raise - I know that sounds wrong, but when you want to set up a trap, this is what you will do on occasions. Calling, then folding, calling then folding, this sets up a rhythm that encourages pot buyers to steal chips.

Each type of player needs a different gambit. Re-raising Old Ladies sets up a rhythm that any hand they play against you will cost. Checking down to a trap player can lead them to believe you are drawing THEM into a trap, particularly if they raise you re-pop (unless they have the goods they fold).

Chasers need nibble bets pre and post flop and an all in (if there are no possible straights or flushes on the table) on the Turn. So many different strategies for so many different players - BUT - you only have a limited number of chips. You have to CHOOSE WISELY. This is where you work with everything we have discussed - the Outs, the Calling Equity, the Pot Value, the Shorts odds and the overall concept of what your IMPLIED ODDS might be.

You don't have too many books speaking about Implied Odds. They are, as the term says, IMPLIED not stated. We use these as a way of resolving our course of action in any hand.

Let's look at a story: We have eight people at a table, under the gun (first to act pre-flop) raises three times the bind. That player is saying they have cards. I have no idea what they have, but this is a solid player and it is most likely AK or AQ - if they hold Aces or Kings I would be in real trouble, because I have woken up with QQ. To my left I see someone ALREADY reaching for their chips.

What do I do? There is no real thought involved - You count the chips, calculate the risk versus the reward - see who else is in the hand and how interested they appear to be - then you act. I am not going to be re-raising because I know Under the Gun will be calling or pushing and beside me is interested. I can see they are the only other one likely to be in the hand, and I do not want to push because I suspect someone may have better than my queens.

My focus in not on the raiser, but the player to my left. I can tell they are definitely calling by the way they have already counted the raise and placed it in front of them. Good players will do this to bait you, by the way - They act as if they are ready to call, whereas they are intending to push or fold. But if they WANT others to call, they make it look that they are only going to call.

In this case, my read is the THIRD player is not a pot buyer, nor an Old Woman, they are more a Trap Player. This person will decide my actions, not the initial raiser. The TYPE of people you play against are all part of your implied odds - In this instance I just call. If the third player has Aces or Kings, they will push. The third player just calls.

Let us stop and recalibrate - why do I just call with Q Q? I have a solid player AND a Trap Player in the hand - this is a TERRIBLE combination to go up against. But also, they have seen me call similar raises with suited connected on that table, so they are NOT putting me on Queens. I want to see a flop but I do not want to risk my stack in the middle of two competent players.

But I also want to get VALUE for my Queens!

WHAT TO DO? You have picked the likely hands you are against. How do you choose a course of action?

ROCK - Raises with AA, KK, AK, AQ

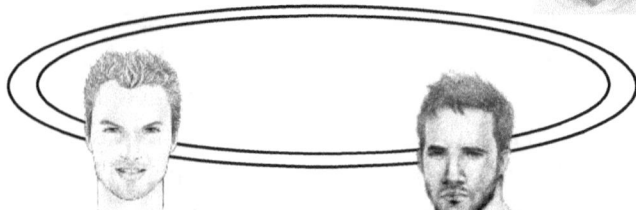

TRAP - CALLS with AA, KK, AK, AQ, any pockets or Suited Connected

YOU - Sitting between these as Second to Act with QQ

After the Flop is where you choose your course. If there is no Ace or King, or obvious flush or straight possibility, and IF the first to act does not push all in, I figure I am 70% certain of being good. So my IMPLIED ODDS say to play the hand in order to maximize my return for investment.

In this instance, a solid raise on the flop, and if no King or Queen by the Turn, then it is All In. Yes, I may have run into Aces of Kings, they may be going slow trying to trap me - you are essentially shooting air whenever you push. But if you DON'T push on the Turn when you believe you are ahead, you have a 62% chance of dying on the river. Why? Whatever you hold - 62% of hands are won on the River.

So, regardless of odds, options or outs - you do NOT want the River to be seen in any hand you are in, unless YOU are the one chasing that card. Even so, if you can outbid the other players at the Turn, do so. At all times encourage people to fold - that is where you pick up chips.

We could spend a book on every scenario - the point of this exercise is simply to get you to think of possibilities and probabilities in any given hand, and to start registering that everything you do is part of a long game. The implications of HOW you act in THIS hand will have repercussions and results in several hands from now.

Earning Respect

Table presence is essential. I was at a Casino with some solid players at my table. I raised with KQ, and got two callers. The flop comes A K 4. As I am first to act, I do a ten times the blind raise. The woman opposite me just calls. The third person folds. I know she has an Ace, I check the next card, she bets, I fold.

You never see a monkey at a poker table, do you? Why? Because they are not good at deceit and they prefer bananas to cash. But offer them bananas, and they are still terrible poker players.

WHY DOGS MAKE LOUSY POKER PLAYERS:

WHODAH! SOUNDS LIKE RUSTY'S GOT A GOOD HAND...

THUMPA! THUMPA! THUMPA!

I flip over the KQ and peoples jaws just drop.

A strong player asks, "How could you fold that?"

I reply, "She has an Ace with a good kicker."

Even the DEALER cannot believe it and, with the agreement of the table, he runs it out. She turns over A J - next card was a J and the river was a nothing. I lost that hand, but EVERYONE on that table played with a great deal more respect after that. Earning respect at any table, establishing a table presence, demonstrating that you are a player to be reckoned with, this will earn you CHIPS.

Nothing earns more respect than a good lay down and a correct read. Nothing puts the fear of the Poker Gods into someone hearts than a person who appears to be able to read what cards another player holds. And I have played with them - people who say, "You are raising with J 10 suited in position, and I have King Rag - but I am ahead and so I am pushing."

I folded, showing my J 10, and he flipped over his King rag.

Know your Odds, know your Outs, and just figure on 2% per card as your value. This is sufficient math to work out most hands quickly. But most of all, know the PLAYERS at your table. This is the thing that earns you the most chips.

And always remember what Paul Newman said, *"A dollar won is twice as sweet as a dollar earned."*

How Many OUTS Versus EVENS for 4 3 Diamonds?

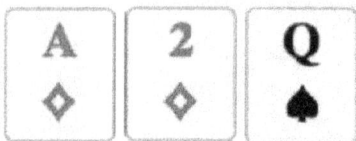

| 4 ♦ | 3 ♦ | | A ♣ | Q ♣ | | A ♥ | 2 ♥ |

| A ♦ | 2 ♦ | Q ♠ |

4 3: Any FIVE - Any DIAMOND = 12
A Q: Any ACE - Any QUEEN = 4
A 2: Any TWO = 2

EXCEPT: Queen Diamonds kills 4 3
Collected EVENS against 4 3 = 6
So: 4 3 Outs v's Evens is 12 - 6 = SIX

NOTE: Only FIVE Diamonds on the Turn will stop the risk of a paired board.

Opportunity Creates Luck

"Poker is a lot like sex, everyone thinks they are the best,
but most don't have a clue what they are doing!"

Dutch Boyd

The Gods of Luck and Opportunity smile most kindly on those who respect them. You have all heard the saying, "Don't push your luck!" and this is very true. Luck likes to be welcomed and embraced, never pushed.

The greatest single mistake poker players make is they focus on LUCK, not OPPORTUNITY. Luck is fickle whereas Opportunity occurs again and again on a regular basis. Luck is finding that rare oyster that holds a Pearl - Your opportunity is planting the seed that grow the pearl and this opportunity arises via awareness and knowing who is at your table.

When you have a good feel for the type of player present, you can play and bet with a reasonable degree of confidence, To a lesser player, your CONFIDENCE is read as Luck.

However, we all know tournaments are a grind. Especially when you have been running cold for three months and every big hand you get dies to someone playing garbage, you can start to doubt yourself and second guess your betting. A little secret - you do not HAVE to be sitting at a poker table. You can walk away, get a drink, breathe in fresh air, and reset your compass. OR you can play for Opportunity, not luck!

Luck comes and goes, but opportunity comes again and again. DO NOT PLAY FOR LUCK! *Pray for it, do not play for it.* When we are having a bad run, we often keep betting because we think we can buy our way out of this hole. WRONG. Other players know when someone is running black and they just call you - For one, you don't have the chips to push them away, and two, you are on a losing streak. Play to Opportunity!

Small positional bets and keeping up with the conversation let people know you are there. These are the keys to moving past the down cycles. If people feel they LIKE you, they go a little easier in a hand they call.

Yes, they will still happily take your chips - that is poker - but they won't call your All In on a two card runner runner draw. Never doubt how some player will call you simply because they don't like your attitude. I have done it, where some dumb or arrogant guy is betting big, buying pots but looking unlucky - I will call him with SFA and see if I get lucky.

You MAKE luck when you SPOT Opportunity. What shuts down Opportunity? Arrogance, stupidity, impatience, these are all an attitude that creates bad vibes and people start to call to be rid of you. Yet you can be cocky and smart arse, but stay playful, and people like it. The vibe you put out, your sense of confidence, the notion you are actually interested in other people at the table - all this paints a picture.

And the picture it paints is your Window of Opportunity. Let's say that people have a basic respect or fear of you, either is appropriate, at a table. You bet, no one re-raises. You bet again, still just a few calls. The table is telling you they have nothing much OR someone is lying doggo. But ANOTHER bet on the River, and everyone folds. This is CREATING your Opportunity by reading the table. It looks to the other players like you got lucky - but you may have held nothing and just bet.

There is also a TIME to create opportunity. When you have been going for 14 hours solid on poker tables you can start to get a little loopy. People are patiently waiting for the opportunity to arise where they can call the pre-flop raises. But when the Flop doesn't look good, and someone is betting, they already feel they have lost. THEIR bad luck is what you make YOUR Luck. This is your OPPORTUNITY speaking.

Real Opportunity is when someone hits, but you are better - *No point having trips when your opponent has nothing* - The LUCK is when a player hits two pair, thinks they are good, and does the betting for you.

So! This guy is at your table. He looks at his cards and bets a min raise Under the Gun. What is your read? He looks like a nerd fresh from the office, easy meat most will think.

This is rarely the case, super conservative looking people tend to play super conservatively and you are maybe running into a monster. Then you notice his messy chip stack. Sure sign of irrationality. He really MIGHT be easy meat!

So you watch how he plays and you WANT to see the River, so you see what he is playing with!

SUMMARY

"The immortal gods are wont to allow those persons whom they wish to punish for their guilt sometimes a greater prosperity and longer impunity, in order that they may suffer the more severely from a reverse of circumstances."
Julius Caesar

When we can read who is at a table and we know our odds, we can make our BETTING a LANGUAGE. The coin we flip is a BET. We can be 'telling' people what we have, while listening to their response. In this way, poker is a dance. Everyone makes their steps according to the song they are hearing.

The hard part is first understanding the song in THEIR heads and, after this, getting them to start singing to YOUR tune. You do this through the art of betting, conversation, and listening. You bring people into your orbit by HOW you act. You get them singing YOUR song by HOW you bet.

Poker is a SOCIAL experience and the truly successful players are not obnoxious or ignorant savages, they are quiet and attentive players who look for opportunity as and when it arises. And when it does, the "flat-eyed predators," as Molly Bloom describes them, start to emerge.

The game is about controlling your table in whatever way works for you, but conversation, betting and looking for opportunity are the hallmarks of all good poker players. It is a WAR disguised as an outing.

If we are too focused on our own mind and thoughts, we will never see the opportunities right in front of us. A greater part of the secret to discovering Luck is knowing when it crosses your path!

Creating Opportunity is what makes Luck. By knowing our Odds, working and shifting the tides to create options, we will see the Window of Opportunity open and we duck through to get our well-earned luck. Any way a player wants to do this is good - We all have our own way of playing the game, but if we adjust our mindset as one of looking for OPPORTUNITY rather than wishing to LUCK we will gain a lot more chips in far fewer hands and for a whole lot less risk.

I absolutely endorse the following webpage as a way to create luck through opportunity in your life:

https://www.entrepreneur.com/article/286336

Section Three

Finding Your Poker Angels

The Strategies that Create
Luck and Opportunity

- Playing High Percentage Hands

- Playing Strategies

- Playing Position

- General Roundup

General Player Strategies

I n this section we will look at specific strategies and why you might play them. A Poker Strategy is like a specialized club in golf - you use it in specific situations for specific ends.

There are many books and online tools to qualify the value of any given hand, so we will limit this section of the basic plays and strategies that come up in every tournament.

Always remember, no matter the cards you receive, if you choose to play them, you must play them to attain a maximum return. This is why pro's will occasionally call a large raise with Ten Eight - They are in position, maybe they have picked the player as emotionally weak at that point, maybe they have picked them as betting with Ace High or maybe they are just feeling lucky!

Odd Statistics against A A

A♣ A♠ V's 9♦ 8♦

9 8 suited is 22.5%
A A is 77.2%
Simple and Clean

A♣ A♠ 9♦ 8♦ 5♥ 6♥

9 8 suited is 20.34%
A A is 59.1%
5 6 Suited is 20.38%

Q♣ K♣

BUT add K Q Clubs - KQ is at 15.6, 9 8 is at 19.2, 6 5 is at 20.59 while Aces are now at 44.53% to win. Yet, the AGGREGATE percentage against A A is now over 55%!

Playing to FOLD EQUITY

The beautiful thing about poker is that everybody thinks they can play.
Chris Moneymaker

What do you bet on this sort of Flop against A Q Diamonds?

Not a lot. There are SO many unbeatable hands you might be running into. Straights, flushes, pockets - Even 8 Clubs J Spades puts you at 35%

Pessimism and paranoia are fully justified in Poker. If something CAN go wrong, it will. Here we discuss playing to FOLD if you have to. It is called *Playing to Fold Equity*.

Very few people consider playing NOT to win, but in a table where you have a lot of callers (As is often the case with online poker) you have to shift your focus from WINNING to SAFETY. Why? Because if four people are calling your 'All In' bet, you will most likely lose.

Playing for your Fold Equity tells a table that you are a careful player, but it also sets up a routine where there will be people who think your small bets represent weakness. They are just waiting to have something so they can push 'All In' and make you fold.

The thing is, if someone is calling a raise, they are calling for SOME reason. They might simply not believe you, they may need a card, or a suit. You don't know WHY they are in the hand, but if they are there it generally means they are drawing to a chance to beat you.

There are many factors that determine your Fold Equity. Who is at the table, what is your position on the table, how deep into the tournament are you? Without going over every scenario, if you believe you will be called, for whatever reason, it is unwise to push with an 'All In'. If you firmly believe the people at the table will call you, no matter the raise, you need to play for Fold Equity - How much can you bet that you can afford to let go if the River is unfavorable?

It is not complicated. I generally recommend that if there are flush and straight chasers in a hand, you VALUE BET the flop, and PUSH the Turn. But if you cannot get them out - if you believe they will call anything - you are betting your tournament on THEIR Luck.

The reality is, if your table presence is strong, if your betting is right, you have set people to wondering that even if their flush comes, will it be good? An 'All In' bet is read by some players as weakness, and they will call BECAUSE of it, especially if they are chipped up and will not be crippled to miss their card.

This is a MAJOR consideration in determining your Fold Equity. It is not just what leaves YOU in the tournament, it is the risk to the opponents stack. Is risk is low, and the opponent is a little loose, they will call whatever you bet. So bet enough to signal you have cards, but leave enough so you are not crippled should they get lucky.

The ONLINE Question: *The new elephant in the room is On Line play. Someone can be sitting on their phone, drinking beer, and can just re-buy into any game or move to a different game. In this story Fold Equity becomes an essential consideration.*

When someone has a flush or straight draw playing an On Line game, they will call anything. There is little risk to fail and a great deal to win.

The PROBLEM when playing to Fold Equity is you risk being charged at on the River. What do you do if the third diamond turns up and they push 'All In'? This is the negative to playing this way. Well, you have played the game to fold if this happened. By signalling your intention to players at the table, you leave yourself open to this sort of action. You may fold and they show a busted straight draw, or they may have gotten exactly what they want.

But here comes the real secret - This is ALSO how you play when you have the NUTZ. You act as if you are worried about cards to come.

So many times I have played what looks like a game of Fold Equity, waiting for someone to jag a straight or a flush. It is especially sweet when the person pushing the River finds you call with the Nuts and they flop over a complete miss.

Playing to Fold Equity is something TIGHT players do. If you want to appear like this, play few hands and raise in small nibbles. If you do this well, better players will notice and you will tend to only get the loose aggressive ones in your hand - which is what you WANT when you have premium cards.

Poker is a Game of Detachment

"The cardinal sin in poker, worse than playing dead cards, worse even than figuring your odds incorrectly, is becoming emotionally involved."
Katy Lederer

Many people have said the real skill in winning is knowing when to fold. This is true, but knowing you probably SHOULD fold, and actually doing it can sometimes be very different animals.

When all is said and done, *Poker is a game of Detachment*. But it begs the question: *How do you KNOW when to hold 'em or when to fold 'em?* How can you feel a sense of certainty in any action, in any hand, at any time? The secret is understanding that the hand was not over when you fold the cards, it was over before you picked them up!

To explain: If you do not have the attitude of detachment in place before you start any hand, any game, any season, you have already lost. If you are not free from your hand, from your hopes and wishes, from your dreams of glory, these things will hang on to you like dead weights.

Expectations pull you down. Hope and wishing for luck only slows your game. Doubting yourself, suffering through a losing streak, bemoaning the fact that cards are not falling for you - these are only proof you did not start on the right foot - Whenever you start with dreams you will end with nightmares.

A good poker player approaches playing a tournament in the same way a builder approaches building a house. They see everything that can go wrong, where costs might blow out, in short - a good builder approaches things with a NEGATIVE attitude, and yet, they also KNOW they can and will build that house.

The successful poker player knows all about the bad beats, and EXPECTS them. A good poker player KNOWS they will get donkeyed, but instead of getting angry or wanting to get even, they laugh and say "Well played!" to the Donkey, because they EXPECTED this. A good poker player on a bad run becomes MORE patient - they do not bet on the first two decent cards they get trying to buy a pot - why? Because they understand that the exact wrong time to push is when other people are running lucky and when you are not.

Luck will turn up if you play the odds, play the players, work your opportunities and keep your patience strong. A detached attitude means you have let go of your problems BEFORE THE GAME STARTED. You KNOW opportunities will come, but you also know they will go.

The DETACHED OBSERVER is the most difficult player to beat. They do not get trapped in the madness that occasionally descends on a table, when all these people start raising and re-raising. They do not buy into the emotional stress of the ups and downs, because they chose not to before the game started.

When you find a state of pure detachment, you realize it is the opposite to what most people think it is. It is being completely and totally involved in the moment, yet free of the need to own it. The purpose of detachment is to free you from fear. It is not to free you from consequences, it is to set you apart from expectation and hope.

Hope is the ENEMY of the poker play. Hoping for something means you pay money hoping it will arrive. Detached play has no use for hope - what it NEEDS is intention. We need to grow any sense of hope we might possess into something far greater, the power of Intention.

When you go into a hand, you go into it Intending to win. This is more powerful, more focused, and people can FEEL it. They KNOW you are in a hand, and they already know that it will be expensive. But if the flop is terrible, and someone bets back at your continuation raise, you are detached enough to let it go.

Detached means turning on a dime. You go in with a plan, but switch gears when required. It means not needing to look big and tough and brave or staying in a losing hand because you have to prove something. It means feeding the ducks, making small talk, not getting caught up in moods or a sense of anticipation. ALL of this creates a sort of invisible shield, where people cannot easily get a read on who you are, how you play, or what you hold.

"No matter how much you may want to think of Holdem as a card game played by people, in many respects it is even more valid to think of it as a game about people that happens to be played with cards."
Phil Hellmuth

Playing the ACE CARD

"Ace-king is a fine hand. Ace-queen is a little weaker, but still good. With ace-jack, you're already sliding rapidly down a slippery slope. With ace-ten, you've slid down the slope, fallen off the cliff, and lie in wreckage at the bottom with hands like ace-five and ace-six."

Dan Harrington

So many poker players give a small smile when they see an Ace. These cards seem to give people an unjustified confidence and yet, because they bet in so hard with one, they CAN cause the winning cards to fold pre-flop. In this regard, they have value.

Where Aces-Rag does NOT have value is when there are five or more people at a table. If you do a large raise and you get called, the odds say there will be a pair or a better Ace and you are playing to a single card. However, when there are four or fewer players at a table, your Ace-Rag is strong - equal to middle pockets in value.

TEST: Which hand has the highest percentage to win?

Trick Question: A7 is a better starting hand, regardless of the greater number of possibilities Ace Suited Connected gives you. Your A 7 has a 44.8% chance to win over A3 suited with just 28.5%

The REAL question is one of where you are positioned on the table and how can you present a winning bid on the FLOP! PARADOX: Queen Nine Suited has a much higher percentage of winning

Heads up, Ace Rag is VERY strong. Let's run the odds - fifty two cards in a deck - four cards dealt and you have an Ace - that is a three in fifty two chance that the other person has an Ace - or 5.67%. Add to this the chance they have pockets, which is 6%, and you are ahead by 88% in any pre-flop bet. Let's run a scenario:

You bet HARD to reduce callers. However, FIVE people call the hand. This equals 5 x 12% against, or 60%. Now, even if you HIT your Ace you cannot be certain it is good. If you bet hard and two call, you can almost be certain at least one of those callers has better than your Ace Rag.

FOUR up in a hand gives 52% your way - acceptable enough for a post-flop raise to see where you stand. But if you ARE going to raise with your Ace, perhaps consider that Ace through to Five is better than Ace Six through to Nine, because two low cards can make a straight on the flop. You have a 2.4% benefit with connected cards.

BUT THE REALITY CHECK! The LOGIC of playing Ace Rag rarely matches the romance of catching a pre-Flop Ace, but if you ARE going to play them, you need to drive the table to a maximum of two callers. You will be trying to BUY the hand on the flop following your pre-flop raise, which is really the ONLY rationale for playing Ace Rag.

Alternatively, you are in the dealer position or near to it, and the entire table has limped in. Then you would consider calling the blind, and NOT raising. Why? Chances are that Under the Gun has called with way better than your hand. If there are any serious raises in front of me, I will generally fold Ace Rag quickly and easily.

Think of these cards is terms of calling with low pockets. The more people in the hand, the far worse your odds get to picking up the pot. But at least with small pockets you CAN flop the world and chip up massively. No matter WHAT you hit with Ace Rag on the flop, unless you hit BOTH you are not in good shape to pick up a big pot.

This is the other thing, when you START with uncertain cards, even if you hit you are not in a position to build a pot. And the only reason you should be IN a pot is to gain maximum value from cards. Even as I say this, I have won tournaments on Ace Rag, but this is because I was heads up on a Final Table against someone pushing with K Q or similar.

As with EVERY poker hand, position is a primary consideration, and your knowledge of the other players at the table makes up the difference between calling raising or folding Ace Rag. So do you play Ace Rag? Of course, but you do so CAREFULLY.

How do you Play THIS on the TURN?

A♣ Q♣

4♠ 5♠ 7♣ 8♣

3♥ 6♦

10♦ A♦

J♠ 10♠

THE FLOP: 4 5 7 SPADES

3 6 has flopped the straight and is ahead.
J 10 has a Flush Draw and a runner runner
straight and straight flush draw.
A Q needs runner runner clubs
A 10 is OUT of the running

The PERCENTAGES to WIN

FLOP	TURN
A Q = 5.5%	A Q = 22.5%
A 10 = 0%	A 10 = 0%
3 6 = 53%	3 6 = 47.5%
J 10 = 40.5%	J 10 = 27.5%

This is where the betting gets interesting. A Q has been driving the betting, 3 6 just called, allowing the pot to build, but NOW they have questions - Are THEY the ones behind? Is someone holding 6 9? Are they drawing dead?

Can anyone confidently PUSH here? No, but with just one card to some, even though J 10 IMPROVED with a higher Straight Draw, it's odds to win are half that of the existing straight. The only cards dropping out are the A 10, everyone else is in with a shot. This run out has 3 6 wishing they pushed on the FLOP and not looked for value.

Should 3 6 check it down? This is a classic situation that depends on where you are paying and who you are playing with. In On-line play, you would min raise, check it through, or call it down. Why? Because everyone bar A 10 will call you anyway. If it holds it holds.

At a table you would PUSH. You cannot buy back in, but neither can they. If you are strongly ahead on the TURN, in real life games you SHOULD be pushing and NOT seeking value.

PLAYING PAINT

"Forget about a chip and a chair;
give me a hand and I'll stand."
Warren Karp

You peel up the cards and that beautiful paint is looking back, saying, *"Kiss me you fool!"* K Q suited is a great start hand, anything painted and suited is good, but how good? What are they really worth and how best to play them are the questions in my mind when I see these.

I know people who push All In with KQ suited, I know people who call all in's with KJ or QJ. This is not smart, unless you are not damaged to lose. Ace Rag is ahead of you. KQ Suited is 43% against A3 Suited at 56%. Yet if we add 77 into the mix, QK goes ahead of A3. It's a curious thing, when you hold painted cards, the MORE people in a hand that you can get into it cheaply, the better value the Pot becomes and the better percentage you have of picking it up.

It goes against all logic, but that is how percentages can turn out. This gives you a clue on how to play paint - softly. Tread softly amidst the noise and haste, etc. When I have suited connected high cards I would consider calling a three times the blind raise heads up, depending on what type of player is doing the raising. But if I am at the end of a chain that has called, you can't keep me out of it.

Do I raise with them? In position, if everyone is limping, yes. If someone raised before me, no, I just call. My personal hatred are for cards like K J because they are behind just about everything that is raising, but I will still call because they are painted and with a favorable flop they can win huge pots.

Will I fold them post flop if they don't hit? If someone is raising and there are more than two people in the hand, I rarely pay to see more than the flop unless I have hit. The thing is, when paint HITS, it tends to create monster pots, When they don't, they can cause monster losses. So, painted cards are excellent for seeing a flop, and that is all.

Post-Flop - they can be monsters or chip sinks - but no one got a royal without them.

PLAYING HIGH POCKETS

"May the flop be with you." **Doyle Brunson**

Heaven on a stick! You look down and see KK or AA! You know you are massively ahead of EVERYONE at the table, but we also know how a Flop can destroy our dreams. How do you play these pearls from the Poker Gods in a way to both capitalize on your good fortune yet cover your bases?

Well, you need to decide before you do anything HOW you will play this hand. Will you trap? Will you min raise? The answer to this is NOT the cards you hold, but WHO is at the table and WHERE they are seated.

PRE-FLOP: Obviously, if last to act is a Pot Buyer, you want to just call and let them do the work for you. If you have a Trap Player looking with interest at their cards, you must raise strongly. If you have a few Chasers you NEED to get them down to one or two, so a strong raise that will leave you with one is ideal. Donkeys call anyway, you just trust that their luck is not running for them.

The one thing we must seek to avoid when holding Aces or Kings is multiple callers. Your odds of winning plummet with four or more in a hand. When I am OUT of position in the Blinds and get Aces, my favorite gambit is a four times the blind pre-flop raise, then I use my poor position as a weapon. I push ALL IN BLIND as soon as the first burn card hits the table. I am telling everyone I have Aces, blatantly, and risking that they didn't jag two pair or similar.

On Final Table, why would you push with AA or KK? You WANT a caller, and looking weak is what you want. If anyone hits anything, they tend to push. This is what we all want, someone pushing when they are behind. However, most people leave a tournament on their AA or KK. Pre-flop monsters can very quickly become post-flop nightmares. EG: You see three of your suit on the flop and someone is raising massively - you have to call, you are drawing to the nut flush.

Try to remember, High Pockets can quickly become a trap for YOU. Calling to a dangerous flop or a potential straight on the board is the reason so many people walk from tournaments with them.

PLAYING SUITED CONNECTED

"It never hurts for potential opponents to think you're more than a little stupid and can hardly count all the money in your hip pocket, much less hold on to it."
Amarillo Slim

Most players like to see suited-connected cards and with good reason - ANY suited-connected are at 22% against anything another person might hold. What this means is that they are not cards you really want to play heads up against a big raise, but they are excellent for calling raised pot with four or more players.

Connected cards are ANY TWO CARDS you hold that can make a straight on the flop. In Texas Holdem, connected cards have a bonus as the chances for a straight are significantly higher than with five card stud because you have an extra two cards to make your hand.

Close connected are cards that are next to each other, 7-8, J-10, etc. Connected means any two cards that make you a straight on the flop. Suited-Connected means you also draw to a flush. CLOSE Suited-Connected cards are some of the most playable in Texas Holdem.

Poker Fact, the hand that most often beats Aces is 5 6 suited. It sits close to 23% pre-flop as odds go, that is a one in four chance of beating the best pre-flop cards you can get. You can hit a flush, a straight, plus you also KNOW the person betting big has high cards. This means with a high card flop you can leave easily. This is the important point: *You are not in DIRECT COMPETITION with the heavy pre-flop raising cards.*

With suited connected cards you are in the LOW RENT district and arguing for different real estate. It is a very defined landscape you need to see on the flop. I promise you, I have not just won a LOT more chips with 3 5 suited than K J - I have also LOST far fewer chips with them.

How to PLAY them is a book all on its own, but you really have to trust your gut instincts when playing with such live cards. The flop will make or break them, so are they 'All In' cards?

Not really. Unless you are bluffing, suited connected pre-Flop are CALLING cards. You have all heard that J 10 is the best hand in poker? Common mistake - they are the best CALLING hand in Poker. Why? Because you can make SO MUCH of them AND if someone hits their high cards, you are still in the running.

| J ♠ | 10 ♠ | V's | A ♥ | K ♦ | *J 10 Suited = 41%*
A K = 58.6%
There is only an 18%
difference between them! |

This surprises most people - What look like vastly inferior cards are so close in value to A K pre-Flop, but that is how it works out. But let us look at another person in the hand. Pockets NINES comes into the pot!

| J ♠ | 10 ♠ | A ♥ | K ♦ | 9 ♦ | 9 ♣ | *J 10 Suited = 32.5%*
A K = 37.1%
9 9 = 30.1% |

Wow! Almost even to AK now! Can you see why they are such good CALLING CARDS? The thing is, with a bad flop and you can get away. But get a GOOD flop and it will suit A K, so they will be betting into you. All suited connected cards can stand a three times the blind pre-Flop raise - J 10 / J Q / Q K suited can easily call four times the blind, PRE-FLOP.

If Suited-Connected cards run for you on the Flop, they can earn MASSIVE pots. This is why professional players love them and call your large raises without hesitation when they hold ones they like. You look at the cards above and it is hard to imagine J 10 has ANY chance at all. Why the odds say A K is ahead of 9 9 is a mystery to most - but this is what the odds say.

The REAL BEAUTY of Suited Connected is that if there is a poor flop, it can leave without second thoughts. With 9 9 you are almost ALWAYS having to call A K raising the Flop, and even if A K has not hit, there is a QUEEN there, or something above your Nines. It is hard to fold, he might be doing exactly what you think he is doing, raising with high cards. So Suited Connected have high value PRE-FLOP, and they are easy to walk away from POST-FLOP. Kind of dream cards, really.

These are tournament winning cards and only a fool to throws them away to a small raise.

GUT INSTINCTS

The key to No-Limit... is to put a man to a decision for all his chips.
Doyle Brunson

I know very few successful poker players who do not trust their gut instincts. There is no reason for some of the calls the leading professionals make, it almost seems they are insane. But as Doyle Brunson proved when taking down the 1976 WSOP championship, you cannot define nor defeat the instincts you pay attention to.

In the WSOP Tournament, Brunson was heads up in a hand with 10 2 - the flop came down A J 10. His opponent, a non-professional player, is holding Ace Jack and makes a small raise. Brunson calls with his TEN and the Turn shows a Two. Brunson naturally thinks he is good, and pushes 'All In'. Cards are tabled, he is in trouble, then the River is another Ten.

In his own words, *"I had played in every World Series of Poker since it started in 1970. In '76, I was heads up against Jessie Alto. I had just beaten the guy in a big pot; he was a notorious steamer, (gets angry) so, naturally, when he raised the pot, I called him with the Ten spades and Two spades. He had an A-J and hit aces and jacks on the flop, with one spade. I had tens. He bet and I called. When a deuce fell on the turn, I moved in on him. I caught another 10 on the river to beat him!"*

So, despite all the talk of playing junk cards, there was basic and sound logic behind the hand. However, Brunson trusts his gut instinct. Most people only hear the mind chatter, and barely pay attention to anything else. Brunson legendary play was not ALL gut Instinct, there was a logical element involved, but his original CALL was an instinct.

When asked about this extraordinary hand and then the more unbelievable push, he said at the time he was happy with second and he was tired of sitting there. He hit well, he pushed. The thing is the GUT Instinct was to call in the first place. The mind gave a justification: "He was a notorious Steamer," was the rationale for calling, but it was his GUT that said to do it. His mind just gave him a reason.

Call with Your Gut - Bet with Your Mind

This is the secret. There is a small signal that goes to your mind, from the stomach and up the Vagas Nerve into the brain. It is a thing that is easy to miss when you are stressed or tired or thinking too much. This signal originate from the sympathetic nervous system, a large ganglionic nerve mass at the back of the stomach. When people say "trust your gut" THIS is what they are talking about - not your intestines.

The Vagus Nerve - Don't you love that? It seems SO appropriate that this is a pivotal consideration for a gambling game that came out of Vegas. Don't

The Vagus Nerve connects your GUT to your BRAIN

lose your nerve, as they say. *Trust your gut!* It is almost the anthem of the gambler. The PROBLEM with this is that most gamblers lose, which is why Vegas exists. Why? Paranoia, fear and confusion, mostly confuses the signal. The brain's fear of loss drives you to make the wrong calls.

When you get "butterflies in your stomach" this is ENERGY generated in the solar plexus. This complex and highly evolved sensory unit is what is sending this signal to the brain in ways you are certain to notice but which few can interpret properly. THIS is why people lose.

Your eyes see a flop, it has many dangers and someone is raising heavily. Your gut is shouting, "Stay out of this!" but your head is saying. "I have ACES!" and calls. The guy flips a straight and you walk home.

What you are feeling is more than just electrical signals in the nerves. It is the whole body system that has been trained in our earliest incarnations with INSTINCT. It is something that FEELS and REACTS to stimuli you eyes cannot see - Like a dog picks up a scent that tells it that the person in front of cannot be trusted so too does the Solar Plexus collect information from the world around you.

Think of this like a radar dish. Its purpose originated in our earliest evolution, as a way to warn against approaching danger. This 'sixth sense' is a very real thing, but for the most part we have trained ourselves not to hear it. One of the great benefits of playing poker is that you are giving yourself a chance to reconnect to this primal self.

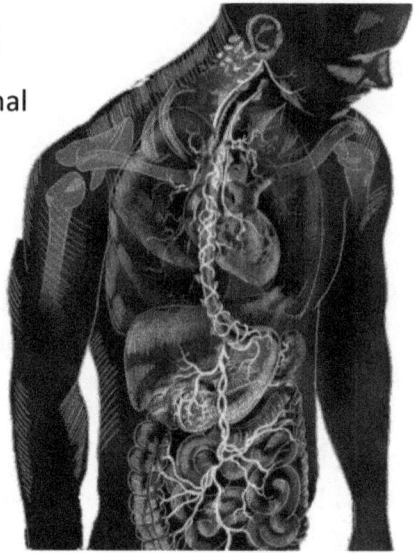

THIS is what starts a persons hands shaking when they are to make a big decision. The entire system is HARDWIRED to adrenalin under stress, which is where the entire science of Tells comes from - observing people under stress.

But while 'tells' are a feast for the eyes, as the last version of Casino Royale pointed out, they can be faked. What cannot be faked is the original gut instinct. The thing that makes James Bond successful can and will work for you, if you have the courage of your convictions.

Make the call with your gut. If you like your cards, if you feel you are good, there is no point arguing over this. See the goddam Flop, and from THERE start letting your mind have a say. Pre-Flop, there really are no odds, despite everything the poker calculators say.

Yes, we all know, over thousands and thousands of hands, the odds will be correct - but RIGHT NOW is a different story. Anything can and does hit that flop. The ONLY real advantage you have Pre-Flop is what your gut is telling you.

Your mind will get the signal and interpret it in any way it likes, such as Doyle Brunson's famous, "Called because he was a Steamer," comment. But the initial impulse, the unconditioned sense of CALL comes from the Gut. Trust it!

The alternative is to play like a robot. Act and raise only on set of internal rules you have given yourself. I know these players, raise on A K or A Q, try and trap with A A or K K - I take their chips all the time. Why? Because they are predictable. This is the other great side to trusting your instincts - you are never able to be calculated by the poker robots.

Your calls seem irrational, your folds seem impossible, but when you fold and you tell the person what they have and they turn over exactly this - by all the Gods of Poker, you watch how differently people play against you. Your table image goes through the roof and your raises are given far more respect.

After that, bluff away! (But read the section on bluffing at the end of this book first)

Real talent is mixing realism with bluff. Every great artist I really respect has a certain amount of bluff; sooner or later you have to be a conjurer, and conjure images.
Terence Trent D'Arby

PLAYING YOUR POSITION

*"The majority of players are looking for reasons to fold.
I am looking for reasons to play." - Daniel Negreanu*

Playing your position is a the fundamental advantage you get in Poker. If you are NOT doing this, you are playing half the game. Your place at any table is like real estate, there are high rent parts of the table, and low rent. If you are sitting in a high rent (dealer Button) and letting low rent players in (Under the Gun) when you hold strong cards, this is a clear and defined flaw in your game.

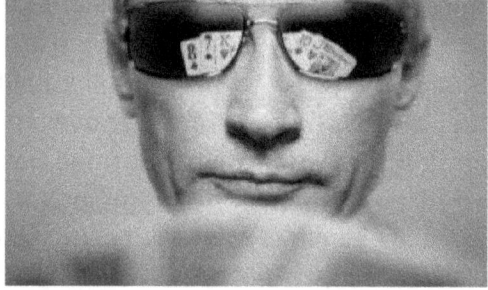

Here we will look at playing position in all the various forms this will take. It is not just playing the position on the table, as in Under the Gun, Dealer Position, etc. it is the *position you put yourself at in the minds of the other players at the table*. It is also the position you are in regards the length of the tournament, where it is a re-buy, etc.

All these tiny details add up to form a massive OPPORTUNITY that others may not see. Poker is ALL its forms is essentially a game of bluff and there are NO two cards you can hold in Holdem that are secure pre-Flop - You use your position to QUALIFY THE TABLE.

Now you don't have to do this with a bet - You can MOUTH your way into people's heads and get reads. But every time you are in a strong position, you should be testing waters in some way. However you choose to do this, it is literally your call - but should most often be your RAISE. If you are in a hand, unless you are in a hand worth raising or that you intend to call a raise should it come, you are playing like every other sucker that gives real players chips.

On the following pages we look at how we might play our position, not just at the table, but in the various stages of the tournament. A small thing most professionals forget. Tournament chips are worth a LOT more than cash game chips - because the blinds relentlessly rise. You have to play position in order to STEAL BLINDS, if nothing else, so that you cover your cost of staying at the table.

LEADING UP to FINAL TABLE

"Money not lost spends the same as money won!" **Steve Badger**

This is one of the most important stages of the game, and playing this correctly makes the difference between winning a tournament, or placing in the low end of the final table. We will presume you have sufficient chips to make it through to the last table. If you play pure safety, you will get there, but in what shape?

More to the point, *this is when most people tighten up* - They are playing to get there, not win. They just want to get to the Final Table, then pray for a bit of luck in the madness that then ensues. This is never a good way to play poker. No, coming up to Final Table is when you are MOST aggressive. This is when you push, shove and push again, because people FOLD. The only serious red flag is a Trap Player limping in.

If you have been tight the whole tournament and you start pre-Flop 'All In" several hands running, EVERYONE presumes you have a monster. Ace Rag FOLDS, K 7 FOLDS. What you get CALLED with are suited connected, or obviously is someone wakes up with big pockets. The fear of losing their seat at the Final, plus your solid play, is what gives you LEVERAGE and this is the time to use it.

If you wait till Final Table to push, you WILL get called. On a Final, low chip stacks will call with any half baked hand they like. If they are two or three tables away, they don't. Yes, I know this makes ZERO sense, but this is why you work this point of the tournament. Even when someone KNOWS what you are doing, they are hesitant to call, just in case.

ALL tournaments I have won have been a grind. Without exception, it was a case of folding reasonable to good hands in the face of adversity - and folding despite the fact that the raiser was pot buying because the THIRD person in the hand looked interested. But in the final stages, *particularly in the extraordinary silence that happens in a big tournament just before players get into the money*, this is the time to be aggressive. THIS is when Pot Buying is particularly effective.

You are playing psychology, not poker, at this stage of any tournament. You CAN be unlucky and walk into a monster, but even then, any OK cards are between 20 to 40% heads up. Trust your Gut, not for your cards, but in recognizing THEIR weakness. And always: *Punish limpers when you are in dealer or next to dealer position.*

Playing the FINAL TABLE

> *There is a tide in the affairs of men, which taken at the flood,
> leads on to fortune. Omitted, all the voyage of their life is bound
> in shallows and in miseries. On such a full sea are we now afloat.
> And we must take the current when it serves, or lose our ventures.*
> **Shakespeare**

Poker is a game of time and tide. As quote says, catching the tide at its zenith is the secret to success. If you are at a Final Table, you have worked your opportunities and created your luck. Now you must capitalize on it.

You can play the Final just like the start of a tournament - buy in when cheap and Small Ball people into folding. The BIG difference between Final Table and the rest of the game is that this is WAY EASIER, because people are running on fear. Everyone is playing to NOT be the next guy or girl out the door.

And when they DO get a great hand, they overplay it - the view is one of getting blinds till you get Aces through to Queens and while this is not wrong, it is just not that profitable. When a person is prepared to play any hand *when in position* they have a huge advantage over cautious players. Position is everything at the Final Table.

If I get Aces, and I am Under the Gun, every part of me is screaming RAISE, but I will generally do a small raise, if any at all. Why? Because someone might just do the pushing for me. Final Table at ANY tournament means the blinds are huge. This qualifies out marginal hands without the need to raise. Remember, we raise to lessen the number of players in a hand. Well, huge blinds DO THIS FOR YOU.

But before you do ANYTHING, stop and breath. This is the time to relax, not tense up like so many seem to do. It is YOUR table, so OWN IT. There is NO place on the planet I prefer than the Final Table of a big tournament. Paris, Rome, London, new York - they are great. But they are nothing compared to the heads up psych control you find at a good Final Table. This is the greatest real estate on the planet to possess and, for myself, it is a place of sheer, unmitigated JOY.

You experience the heights of peoples stress and emotion and no matter how cool someone appears on the surface, under the skin they are bubbling. They have come to the focal point of, in some cases, DAYS of concentration. The Secret: *Make THEIR stress work for you.*

Final Table is where all my stress leaves. This is where I wanted to be. Everything I have done prior has been leading up to this point and now I relax. I breathe in, feel the tension, and savour it like a fine wine. My focus was never on winning, my complete and total effort was zeroed in on being at THIS table. I have succeeded - I am happy.

NOW I focus on winning. NOW there is nothing else in my thoughts. Right NOW I am nothing but a ruthless poker player. There is no thought, feeling or concern about the outside world. I am completely detached from anything but the outcome of the upcoming hand. If I was a smoker, I would be sitting back with a huge cigar sipping a glass of hundred year old brandy.

When the game cranks up, I stop and look at everyone present. I am looking with a huge sense of delight. I LOVE being here. This is my natural HOME. I am an animal designed for this place, it is my natural habitat and I know how to live inside it like no one else.

And what happens? People see me looking bright and happy and they presume it is because I got something. It is NOT deception, I DO have something. In poker, when someone is smiling and cheerful, they are either a fool or dangerous. The fact you are sitting at the Final Table of a major tournament pretty much proves you are not a fool.

Playing Final Table is an opportunity to chip like no other, but if you arrive with only a couple of blinds, what can you do? Any two decent cards means you push - So this is what EVERYONE is looking for. A low chip player who is desperate. I am the opposite, I like to look at the high chip players - why? Because they get careless. They start thinking they are good and call with marginal hands.

You have the perfect opportunity to Small Ball high chip players. If you hit ANYTHING on ANY Flop on a Final Table bet the minimum. They are not fools, they called with King whatever and you may have Ace rag - small bets test them, all the way to the river, where they fold if they do not hit their high card. Your risk is minimal, your gain is enormous.

Final Table is all about LEVERAGE. Every pot is worth winning, because the blinds alone make them worthwhile. Chipping up means chipping away at the main players, who are far more predictable than heads up against the desperate ones.

Now, on this point, people used to be respectful, once, a long time ago. If there were three people in a final table hand, and one was all in, the other two used to sit back and let it run to the river.

This was not just gentlemanly, it made a lot of sense. You really just want a person out. With them gone, your ranking and your cash improves. But this is rarely done now. People are far more aggressive and if they hit anything they are trying to raise you out of the pot so they end up against the All In low chip player.

I cannot tell you the number of times I have said these simple words and cannot even begin to tell you how many times it has put me in the chip lead. *"I was checking it down to be gentlemanly. I had this on the Flop but, as you seem interested, I will see how interested."*

Then I will raise whatever the amount I feel will get them to either call or fold. If I have it, I want them to call, obviously.

Caveat: *You really DO need to have something because a lot of people crack at this point. Even with just a high card they will push back. I have called someone raising into an empty sidepot on a Final with Ace Jack, I had hit nothing. They hit less with Ace Six, or similar.*

Here we are dealing with people who sincerely do not believe they deserve to win. They WANT to, but in their hearts they are panicking. THIS is why someone is arrogant. THIS is why people push. THIS is why people get snarky and upset at your constant nibble bets.

And here is the real truth, the core to the whole secret that is the Black Art of Holdem!

When the torch is applied, what we discover is that 98% of people really do not believe they deserve to win. THIS is why you keep seeing the same names at Final Tables in major tournaments - These are the people who truly believe they DESERVE to win.

Bad beats aside, the difference between winning and losing on the Final Table is a persons deep seated belief in their own self-worth. THIS is why Brunson called with !0 2. "The guy was a known Steamer," or a person who loses their cool. People who lose it believe they deserve to fail and THIS is what Brunson was calling against.

Again, trust your gut. Trust that IT can read the deep seated motivation driving that person better than all your tells. Trust that IT knows something your mind doesn't. In the end, trusting your gut is really believing that you deserve to win. So you don't start a fight with yourself over what to do, *ask if you deserve to win.*

START of a TOURNAMENT

*It's not whether you won or lost, but how many bad beat stories you were able to tell. — **Grantland Rice***

The first twenty hands of any tournament is like the start of a race - a lot of people want to get into the lead and set themselves up in control of the table. You will often find one person prepared to maniac it and risk their game on an early bluff.

You are playing to cash up off the bombers - the ones who splash the chips and trust to luck. The basic technique at the start of a tournament involves not folding your blinds or dealer position. It is as simple as this, call any raise that is less than 10% of your stack with any OK cards. Then, if you jag the Flop, push.

I cannot tell you how many people go out in the first 10 minutes of a major tournament because they raised with AK and called an all in on the Flop. In some ways, I understand it - You are fresh, full of beans, and you KNOW there is hour after hour of endless grind in front of you. If you have good cards and can double up you are in a seriously strong position to play for more chips and be able to relax mid-tournament when everyone is grinding and scratching away.

I also cannot tell you the number of times I have doubled and tripled up in the first few hands of a hundred tournaments. All I did was call a raise in position, and when I hit well I pushed. No science, no clever calculation, just knowing the opponent was behind, but would call.

I cannot ALSO tell you the number of times I have had A A or K K in the first few hands and LOST massive numbers of chips to maniacs. And it is always to people drawing to straights or flushes, or they had Q Q and called my push on the Flop and collected a Queen by the river. Even so, as much as large raises and calls are dangerous, the start of any tournament is a great time to chip up.

Here is the thing to remember - You are also setting up your table image. As a result, this is NOT the time to play every hand. If you do, astute players will see you are loose and punish you with raises.

Front of Tournament is the time to *play your table position* and, at the same time, *establish your table presence.* (Even though you will be moved in an hour or so) There is one basic rule in ALL the low blinds - *Defend your Blinds* and *Play the Dealer Button.*

NEW to Tournament Play

Start of Tournament is essentially the first hour of play, however, if your are allowed a two to four hour grace period before having to start your game, I recommend you take it. The longer you stay out of the game, the less time you have to sit grinding away, the better off you are. And there are several other advantages.

One: New to Tournament Play is powerful. You come to a table where people are more set into the groove of their game and it is much easier to read what you have in front of you. But they have no idea about you, so you can stamp a presence quickly and easily.

Two: In nature, when a new monkey turns up, the existing tribe regards them with suspicion. Same with poker players, people are looking at you more than the others, trying to figure you out. When you push, they have NO idea if you are just buying or you have cards. There is a value in this distraction that you can capitalize on.

Three: Blinds are up, so the dribble callers who play every hand are more conservative. Raises are more effective at reducing the people in the hand. Let's face it, when blinds are 50 / 100 and the stacks are 30K your triple the blind raise is meaningless. Everyone calls it. But when they are 1K and you raise to 3K - this represents ten percent of the start stack and fewer people call.

Four: Low blinds means small pots, which means more hands. High frequency playing in low blinds, even if you are winning, doesn't improve your chip stack much. A hundred hands that win 1K are not as good as three hands that win 30K. What? You think my math is wrong? Yes, you are 10K down, but your RISK FACTOR is negligible.

Remember, RISK is a cost. Not just emotionally, if people see you playing to risk, they will call more often, seeing you are a loose player. *This amplifies your risk in ongoing hands.*

Playing the BREAK

*"A Smith & Wesson beats four aces." **American proverb***

As low chipped players come up to a significant break in any tournament, lunch, dinner, etc. they become reckless. The attitude is "Hell, what's the point coming back to 3K chips? I may as well push and see if I get lucky!" And they DO.

These are good hands to be in, because most of the callers are not in the same boat, and are prepared to check it down to the River. But, as I say, those who play for luck often get it - though it is called bad luck. WHY be in a hand with multiple callers? Unless you have small to middle suited connected you want people OUT of the pot.

Re-Raising the hand against a lot chip desperation bid stops the beggars banquet from forming up. You may be unlucky and run into Aces coming after you, so All In is rarely a good idea - We raise just enough to stop all the callers with any two cards.

But it also runs the other direction - I had a memorable hand where I had been running dry the whole tournament. Three hours in I had just 10% of the start stack and lunch was being called. I am in the Dealer position and watch the callers limping in - the whole table on the 600 blind! This meant with me calling, there would be 4500 in the Pot. If the small blind calls, 4800. The Big Blind has an itchy trigger finger, he is also low chipped. No one looks confident.

I look at my cards and see Aces. A perfect Storm!

"Look people, I have OK cards, but I have been running dry and really don't want to hang about. My tiny 3K is just three times the blind coming back from break, so I may as well push. No point me hanging about with no chips." I get five callers, the Small Blind folds, there is 16800 in the Pot. The Aces hold.

Small Blind shakes his head and shows the 2 5 he folded, which would have given him two pair. Bid 'em out of bid 'em in - It's not your CALL, it's your RAISE that drives the table.

Playing CASH GAMES

*"Poker is not simply a game of odds, moves and calculations.
It is a game of controlled and exploited emotions including
greed, fear, over-confidence and anger."* **Steven Lubet**

Cash games are a different world to Tournaments. It's the same game we are playing, but the WAY it is played is totally different. In a CASH game if you lose your 'All In' push, you peel off some more readies and put them down and you are back in the game. Plus, the blinds don't move - If you sit at a $10 table, that is the Blind for the whole night.

What this means is that you are not being put under the torch to play marginal hands as blinds soar, not are you are not out of the game is things fall the wrong way - You can just buy back in. But this ALSO means people will risk more for a chase and bet more on hitting a high pair. Cash games are not just Casino Tables or private house games, there is a fairly elite high stakes two or three table Tournament circuit which are effectively Cash Games in how they are played.

Getting a read on the type of player is essential in Cash Games, as people play looser and harder. The correct read can win tremendous pots. Further, in a Cash Game, you can walk away with the money at any time. The chips equal CASH. In home games, people often play with actual money.

Did you play poker for matchsticks as a child? Most people who like cards have done this - it seems to be in our genes. A Cash Game is a raw, heads up game of chance where you might be putting a few weeks wages down on the turn of a card. It's adrenalin pumping anxiety for some, the thrill of the chase for others, and a cash cow for a select few.

How do you turn Holdem into a Cash Cow? Tight Aggressive Trap Play works incredibly well in Cash Games and at Casinos. Loose Aggressive Pot Buying works well, but Tight Passive players lose badly.

If you are only playing A K or Pockets you will struggle to make cash at a Casino. Why? Because Cash Game players live off their wits and tend to get a better read on who and what you are. If they KNOW you only raise with A K or Pockets, they have a huge advantage in buying you out of pots after the Flop.

We like to imagine that the higher the stakes, the better the level of play. Sadly, it is often the opposite. High cash tables equals high risk, and real gamblers form up a strong percentage of players.

This is why Tight Aggressive Trap Players can rake in huge sums at these often fairly loose high stakes tables. High Stakes you rate as over One Hundred Dollars as the minimum bet, or a buy-in tournament of over $10K. There is a real chance for a smart player to cash up in these games as there is a lot of bravado - Bravado = dumb calls.

One form of quality Poker is the $1K to $5K buy in tournament. There are a lot of these running in any given town and, in a two to three table game, you tend to get a very high standard of play. You ALSO get a far higher chance of the game being rigged with mechanics for dealers, so only buy into these types of games where you know the people behind it, or you have friends who can vouch for them.

A must-see movie in this regard is "Molly's Game" - based on the true life story of Molly Bloom. At this point, Poker stops being a game and it becomes your lifestyle. Professional gamblers live in the orbit of these games and, without being too harsh, the average fish doesn't stand a chance in a room full of sharks.

But there is a tremendous amount of fun and enjoyment to be had in small stakes Cash Games, plus a goodly amount of pocket money to be picked up. One warning, egos loom large and many people equate winning with self-worth. They can get violent, so it truly pays to play quietly and humbly, and thank people for the cash they give you.

I find it extraordinary how people feel happier when you thank them for their chips. I always say it sincerely and compliment them for their fortitude or courage, or whatever you want to throw into the mix.

Again, a basic warning - It is VERY easy for someone to rig Cash Games and bring in a mechanic. You CANNOT WIN in these situations which is why playing small time private poker dens is a thing to be avoided. This is the great danger in all private games now, you will never pick a good mechanic at work, other than the fact you will never make a profit come the end of the night.

ONLINE POKER

"A Fool and his Money are soon parted" **Anonymous**

This is the ubiquitous game now. The above illustration is typical of the game play - someone pushes ALL IN with 8 2 Diamonds.

Online tables seem to break the odds into pieces and the person pictured above picks up the pot with runner runner Diamonds. Here is the core problem with on-line play - it is much harder to pick the type of person you are up against.

Further: The FREE online games are not as they seem and are rigged to give a lot of 'donkey luck' to players. What they are really doing is encouraging players to be reckless, give them crazy wins, then crash them to zero - This triggers the punter to BUY IN with real money in a FREE GAME to get more chips to splash about.

Facebook games and the like are NOT regulated. They are designed to milk money from players. They encourage manic calls and bets. It HAS spilled over into real life games to some degree, but the main point here is learning to play these crazy on-line games the correct way.

Coming from thousands of these free to play, nothing to earn tables there is an entire new breed of poker player who have compressed thirty years experience into two years, because of the frequency and ease of playing game after game after game. But they haven't really grasped odds or creating opportunity as part of their game.

Because of this, Pot Equity, Value betting, all the basic skills of a poker player are thrown out the window. On-Line play is all about polarized playing - either constant small balling or outrageous over betting. As an exercise, when I started writing this book, I hopped onto a free to play game. Inside 8 weeks I picked up - wait for it - over Two QUINTILLION chips.

Next week, it will all reverse and I will get bad beat after bad beat, as the program is designed to encourage addiction, which then requires you to pay some money to keep it going.

REAL MONEY ONLINE GAMES

The 'real money' online games are regulated as part of the various gambling commissions of the country they are based in, but it pays to be aware where this is. One is headquartered in the Dominican Republic and has next to no regulation. Try getting your money out of these and you discover it is a minute to get the cash in, weeks to get it out.

Even the reputable on-line providers can have issues. Collusion is one, where people who know each other on tables and share information at your expense. People can also easily set up VPN's and put themselves into multiple positions on a table. If someone is covering four seats at a table, they control it.

The other thing about On-Line play - The cards are dealt as a random number generator. Fairly simple simple programming, but unlike actual card games, the numbers are generated at the close of each betting round. This is to make hacking more difficult, but it also means that the next card is 100% random. Eight people in a hand = sixteen cards. A burn plus the flop = four cards. That is twenty cards, with 32 to come.

Here's the difference - the 'burn' is a blank, the number generator is pulling one of 32 cards, not 31, then saying two are gone while putting up the Turn, and calling for one out of thirty. It may not seem like much, but it is. In a real game, the cards that are to come are FIXED - In On-Line play, nothing is fixed. Everything is essentially, *'let's throw the cards into the air and see which ones land face up'.*

What does this mean? Your TURN card is a 1 in 32 chance, not a 1 in 52 chance. In a real life game, every card represents a flat 2% - in ONLINE play, the TURN equals 3.125% - This is a massive difference.

What it ALSO means is that the chance of people getting what they are calling for on the TURN is 55% HIGHER. Does this start making sense, how people so often get what they chase for On-Line but not so much in real life games?

People will dispute this, say that it is all random and that the odds are the same - but they are not. A random number generator has vastly different odds choosing from 32 cards as it does from 52 cards. This is simply mathematics. Yes, you COULD model for a more accurate read, but that would make the whole thing not so random - fiddle the odds and you risk someone fiddling with the game.

Don't laugh - On Line Poker means kids can be millionaires before they finish school

Certain 'reputable' online houses were charged for money laundering. Others ensure their own players get into the higher levels of tournaments. Their paid players do not get the full rake, therefore the house capitalizes by retaining part of the payouts.

Given that Russian mafia owned one of them, we should not be too surprised if things are not as they seem. This is not every online house, there are many reputable companies out there running a fair business.

But the aggression and downright risk taking that the on-line component has added to the game has made it extremely difficult for people to play a solid tournament in real life scenarios. It DOES spill over in the game play and though the gamblers do not get the straights and flushes they pick up on line, they still put a whole lot of good players out of the tournament.

The basics of On-Line play remain, however. Nibble bet, put in constant raises no matter what comes in any hand you are in, and see it to the River. OR, if you have hit a monster, forget about slow play! People call with anything - You still check raise, but then you PUSH.

Yes, you CAN make a lot of money with On Line Poker. So can a five year old with access to a bank account. In the end, the best five cards win and it doesn't matter if they are pixel or paper or plastic ones. The greatest advantage is the obvious, you can play multiple games, multiple blind levels, and all from the convenience of home. In this regard, there are some serious opportunities to pick up quite substantial incomes. On Line Poker is here and it is here to stay.

How to BLUFF EFFECTIVELY

In poker, as in business, the secret is in knowing how to manage risk and capitalize on opportunity.
Lou Krieger

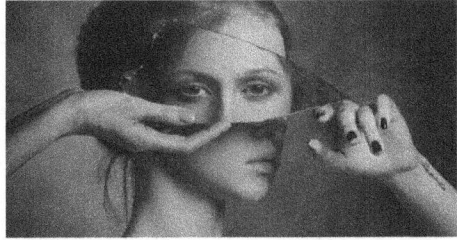

N ow that you have learned all the tricks of the trade, worked out who is at your table, found how easy it is to calculate out your odds, and learned to trust your Gut. Excellent, there is still one thing you need to know and practise and it is the ONE thing precious few ever get right. The Art of Bluffing.

All through this book I have suggested to you over and over that any raise should be posed as asking a question. Now I will stress, it is not the question you ask that matters, but HOW you ask it. We all know WHY someone will bluff, they want to pick up easy chips. We know HOW they bluff, they raise to the point no one wants to call. We know WHEN people bluff, in position, when the table shows weakness, etc. But we have not really covered the process of bluffing effectively.

Raising the ante in some hand is NOT a bluff. Raising without cards is not a bluff. Bluffing is an attitude and it as ancient as the day is long. The German game "Pochen" is an early form of Poker - the word means to "Knock". When you make a your bet, you would KNOCK the table, as if to say "I have this. It is MINE!"

it was both a challenge to the other players to call, as well as a BRAG that you are better than they are. Plus, the physical rapping on the wood was a wake up call, a demand for you to PAY ATTENTION. The whole thing was done in jest but it was also to bluff people out of calling and take the money on the table.

To Bluff effectively, you have to give people the sense that you are knocking that table, demanding them to answer in some way. You are asking if they think they are good, and at the same time, you are TELLING them you are.

But tell me again what happens when a guy goes into a locker room full of Alpha males and starts beating their chest that THEY are the Top Dog in the room? A huge fight ensues because EVERYONE wants to be

Top Dog. *This is NOT the Art of Bluffing.* Creating open conflict on a table only leaves a bloodied mess of one or more people. This is the LAST thing you want, to risk your game in a brawl.

Amarillo Slim said, "You can shear a sheep a hundred times. You can only skin it once." Bluffing is the Art of Shearing Chips. It is not a gun to the head - that is the 'All In' bet. Bluffing well is primarily reading when people are not strong and painting the picture that you are.

It is NOT, "I am the best player in the room" but a quiet claim that you are ahead in this hand. This is why I keep reminding people to voice a bet as a question. ASK if people are interested. A quiet question has more power than a thumping fist, because a question goes into the RATIONAL mind and gets it thinking. An ape-like table thump hits the reptilian brain and activates the fight or flight response in your punters. Some will run, others will decide to NEVER fold.

The Art of Bluffing is very positional. It a form of hypnotism that suggests you are ahead - It is a smile, a confident tilt of the head as much as it is the bet. The secret to bluffing well is to play a hand EXACTLY as if you hold Aces with an Ace on the board. You send a signal there is very little that can beat you, that you are amazingly strong.

When you look people directly in the eye and KNOW you are good you set up a question in the mind of the opponents. Second pair and third pair will not fold to the FIRST bet, Maybe they will call ANOTHER bluff on the turn - but if they have not picked up a second pair by the River, they WILL fold to a good Bluff on the River.

I have even told people, "You should call, I have nothing at all and am just bluffing you off the Pot." If they call, you lose, and you have to show the bluff. But at least you look like an honest liar! Sometimes, even if they fold, I show them the bluff. Why? In another hand when I will do EXACTLY the same when I HAVE cards and they will call.

A small word of advice, if anyone asks, *"Will you show me your cards if I fold?"* ALWAYS say that you will. They are looking for a reason to fold, give them one. And when they fold - push your cards forward, face down, and say, "These are my cards." Then muck them! REMEMBER: *It is about controlling the table, not making friends.*

Yes, you CAN bluff an All In, but this is more desperation than a bluff. Real bluffing creates a mood of anticipation, "Does he have it?". By the end of the day, the person who cannot bluff well cannot consistently win - It is as simple as that. Remember all those guys who always end up on Final Table? *Look at how they bluff if you want to see how they win.*

ROLE PLAYING

The Art of Bluffing is far more effective when you add a little Hollywood into the mix. It helps to PLAY A ROLE at a table. We all need to create a Table Image, and whatever you do is your call, but let's look at some of the most obvious ones.

Playing the Fool: This is when you come to a table acting drunk, or appear as a careless player. The trick is to look like a person who doesn't seem to get the game. You may look like an old, doddery man who has trouble counting chips, whatever the disguise you dress and act in a way that makes the hungry wolves salivate. This is particularly effective in casino games where the local 'sharks' see you as easy meat.

The Woody Allen: Occasionally you see a player who seems incredibly stressed with every decision he has to make. This is a really clever way to hide a ruthless trap player. After a while, players get used to their dithering and their shaking hands indicate they think they are way behind as they call. It really encourages the Pot Buyers to bet big, thinking the guy will have a nervous reaction and fold.

The Helpful Gent: Some players act magnanimous, speaking well of everyone, and looking like they are there to help you. The table image is that of a gentle friend. This type are psychic vampires who live off fresh blood with words like, "Young fella, you seem pretty new at this and I don't want to take your chips, but it is a game of chance, and you may get lucky on the River. I am All In!"

The Sarcastic Prick: Sometimes this isn't an act! There is a type of Poker Player who gets a read by pushing buttons. They insult people, ridicule them, and find ways to drive them to act in the direction they want them to go.

Pretty Thing: SO many girls (and gay guys) do this one. Smile, looking pretty, wear a nice dress and give a hint that you might have a chance. It is all to get your attention of your game and onto them, then they steal your chips while they are fluttering the eyelids.

And countless other variations of disguise. Remember, it is acting, it is HOLLYWOOD to get your chips.

Hoodies, Buds and Glasses

"Show me a good loser, and I'll show you a loser." **Stu Ungar**

How many serious players at a final table do you see dressed up like our friend in the picture? Short Answer: Hardly any. Why? The reasons are very obvious, just as wearing sunglasses, earbuds and hoody's cut you off from THEIR observation, it cuts down YOUR ability to observe. It also kills your greatest asset, your mouth.

Just watch a real pro at a table where there are kids like the one above. One little side look from a Phil Ivey and you KNOW they are dead meat. The pros feed on them like fried chicken.

Would you go and prod a tiger? Turn up to a table of pros wearing all the paraphernalia and you are painting a target on your forehead. Plus, all that 'stuff' cuts down your ability to interact with the table. I was sitting at a Casino - beside me was a nervous guy wearing a hoody and VERY dark sunglasses. I asked him, "Isn't it difficult reading your cards with those sunglasses?"

He looked up and said, "I used to wear reflective ones, but I kept losing. Finally, one of the guy told me they could see my cards in the glasses, so now I wear extra dark ones."

The poor sucker - I didn't laugh. He had no idea that his posture, mannerisms and general sense of losing were far greater signals than anything his eyes might say. Plus, he made himself a target. His lack of confidence was driving his dress choice, not his ability to play. Plus, ear buds in particular cut down on conversation and TALK is one of your greatest weapons on any poker table.

Ashley Adams said, *"I deliberately chat up the player to my left. He's the player, based on his position on me, that I most want to subdue with kindness. He's the one who is most likely to raise after my action. And so he's the one I most want to keep from raising me, by making him my 'poker table friend'."*

Wear what you will to a poker table, but when I see someone all covered up, or pulling their shirt over their mouth, I see weakness and play accordingly. Remember: *Strong players WANT to be seen - they can FAKE tells fairly easily and want you to KNOW they have no fear of you.*

It's Called HOLDEM Not FOLDEM

"Poker's the only game fit for a grown man. Then, your hand is against every man's, and every man's is against yours."
W. Somerset Maugham

Considering you spend most of your game folding cards, you have to wonder why it is called Texas HOLDEM. It is more the ability of a player to pick a bluff and hold their cards that gives the game its name. This is a game of aggression where you have to find the tipping point between playing the hand or waiting for the next set of cards - but the KEY to HOLDEM is that you have NOTHING till the FLOP.

You cannot have a winning hand pre-Flop, unless you drive everyone to fold before a card is turned over. This, obviously, will never win you chips, so the game perhaps would best be called Texas FlopEm? It is a game of resilience where your read of your opponent is far more important than your cards.

On this point, I will share with you what happened when playing a tournament that I won. I was looking across the table at a player and I heard my thoughts saying, 'Not much of a player. Bit of a fool."

This shocked me - I NEVER think this. I NEVER close my book and decide I know what a person is. Looking inside, I realised my fear was taking over. It had been a tough game with too many Bad Beats. Fear was getting leverage in my head and doing my thinking for me. I was somewhat shocked, I thought 'I' was the person doing the thinking!

I did NOT push back with an 'All In' as I was going to do. It turns out my A K 'was' well ahead, but he jagged the card he needed on the River.

The voices in our head whisper many things and the truly deep *Black Art of Holdem* is finding your Poker Angel, then training yourself to hear the still, silent whisper of that voice within, the one that speaks only truth. (Can be hard to hear in the rattle and bluff of betting and booze.)

May that Angel of Fortune guard you and see you right.

The COIN FLIP

In closing, I want to thank you for reading this little book of Poker Wisdom. As a parting comment, there is something that ALL players need to understand - the Coin Flip. In every tournament, at some point ,you will be forced to commit your game to what is effectively a flip of the coin.

You will be in a situation where you cannot fold and you have to blind call All In Pre-Flop. These are unavoidable situations and though we try to never get into this 'pure luck wins' scenario, it is thrust upon us. What I want you to understand is that in any tournament of more than seven tables, a Coin Flip is inevitable.

Rough figures, every seven tables in a Tournament means one Coin Flip. Seventy tables equal TEN all in bets or calls where nothing is certain. You either survive these or you don't and it is FAR better to be the person DRIVING the action than the person calling it.

Why? Because if you are the one pushing, the others are forced to choose if this is THEIR Coin Flip. The other thing, it doesn't matter what cards you hold in any pre-Flop total commitment. (most Coin Flips happen in the Pre-Flop action) You might have raised with Pocket Tens, then someone following you pushes All In. Your raise meant you are crippled to fold, so you have to call. It is better to make the decision before someone makes it for you. And simple advice: If you are not going to call an All In, fold before it starts.

Let's say you play and he turns Q J. It is great to be ahead when the cards turn over for the showdown, but with five cards to come, anything can happen and usually does. This situation is exactly what you want to avoid, but when you are at a point of no return, there is nothing else to do. However, if you think it likely someone WILL push in the hand you are interested in, it is better that you initiate the action.

For one, it limits the number of people calling. With luck, when you go All In, and the next guy pushes with a massive stack so everyone else is on notice that a missed call means they are out of the game. That way you are heads up, which is your best outcome.

I close this book on the Art of Holdem with a small thank you for reading it. Over, I include a prayer to the Poker Gods that you may want to remember and say on odd occasions, as appropriate.

Prayer to the Poker Gods

Our Game Which Art From Texas
Hold 'Em Be Thy Name

Thy Cards May Come, Thy Blinds Be Done
At Home Games As It Is In The Casinos

Give Us This Day Our Daily Chips
And Forgive Us Our Suck Outs
As We Forgive Those
Who Suck Out Against Us

And Lead Us Not Into Bad Calls
But Deliver Us From Bad Beats

For Thine Are The Flop
And The Turn And The River
For Ever And Ever

ALL IN

EPILOGUE

WHEEL OF FORTUNE

The Wheel of Fortune, the endless round of chasing, achievement and loss. The trick to staying on the top is to drive the wheel, not be driven by it.

S uffice to say, everything you have read is tried and true, and half of it is wrong. No matter what hand you are in, no matter how you play it, no matter how good your read - there is always a spanner in the works. No book can give you the instincts and ruthlessness needed to win consistently, nor can it guide you through the mire of depression, bad beats and losing streaks that can, and do, come our way.

What is the overall truth is that things come in waves and that, if we catch that wave and ride it, our life will be better for this brief moment. My only real advice is to be free, enjoy the sunshine, and to live for that moment. If you are coming from a start point of freedom you are already ahead of everyone else at your table.

How so? No matter what happens in the next hand, you already have every-thing you need. Fear cannot control you, doubt cannot assail you, you are Nietzsche's archetypal superman. If you are strong in your sense of who you are, it gives you a presence. People pay more attention to you - THIS gives you an opportunity to capitalize on their curiosity.

There is so much more I would love to tell you regarding Texas Holdem, but in the end it is simply spotting weakness and capitalizing on opportunity. But first you have to SEE this! It is a game of observation and gut instinct. It is a game of knowing the type of player in front of you, and how they might react to your action. And yet, at the same time, it is a game of sheer, dumb luck. The trick is to still be there when that luck strikes! Happy betting folks.

The BLACK ART of HOLDEM

Copyright 2020 Ladder to the Moon Publications
Publisher: Ladder to the Moon Productions
Email: qrcaustralia@gmail.com
Web: laddertothemoon.com.au

By the Same Author

A virus, transmitted by light that attacks your MIND is discovered on a newly settled world. It threatens to take over the Human species in ways too horrible to imagine.

The WOLVES of PLANET HOPE

I t was a shocking discovery, one no-one had suspected. A DNA modifying virus that can be spread with light! Worse, it specifically affected humans and turned them into crazed beasts. Whatever it was on this planet only one thing was certain, it was a threat equal to that which wiped out Old Earth!

It is the Twenty Seventh Century. Mankind has spread out over the galaxy, dominating many worlds in what is called the Federation. But was this one world too far?

Planet Hope, the latest project for the human expansion, is home to a friendly pack of humanoid wolves. They seem entirely welcoming, but soon after settlement, disturbing events required the intervention of the feared Death Squad. A dangerous infection has been found and must be dealt with.

The leader of the squad, Lieutenant Josh Banner, discovers this is no ordinary exercise - He has to assess and deal with a potential threat to ALL humanity, not just the settlement on Hope. Banner looks at the facts and expects only one conclusion - a whole lot of what his squad was named after.

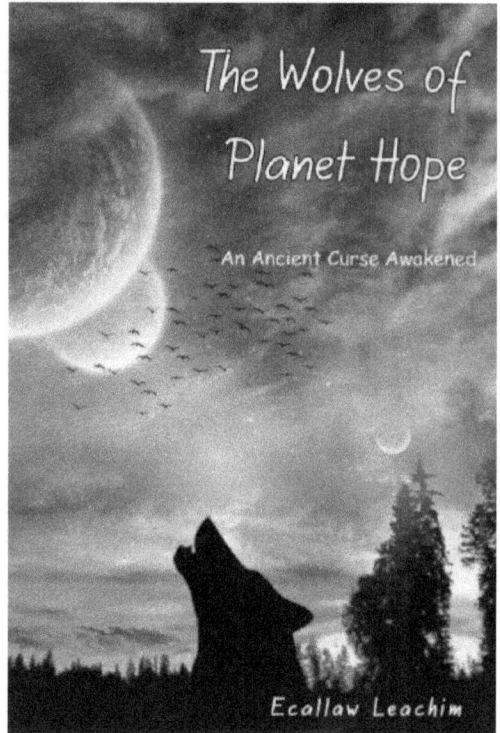

Available on Amazon or at www.laddertothemon.com.au

"Brilliant - Old Fashioned Sci-Fi at its best!"

The WAND
Ecallaw Leachim

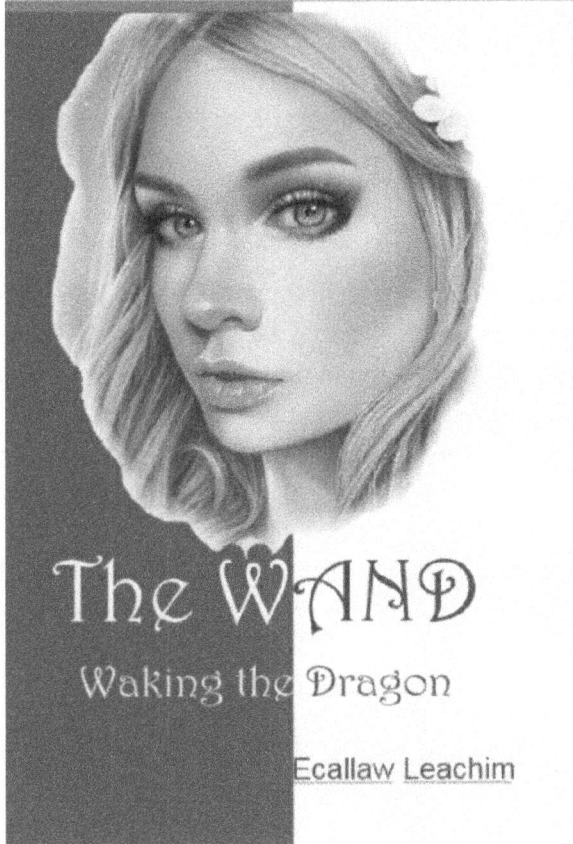

The WAND
Waking the Dragon

Ecallaw Leachim

A Celebration of Wonder and Fantasy. The WAND is a book that lightens the heart and brings joy into your day. Under the fabric of this modern world, an ancient civilization of Elves exists in a dimension beside us - It is a place controlled by magic, but which is threatened by the development of nuclear weapons.

In order to save themselves and the human race from the destruction about to reign down, a small party of ancient ones cross the great divide to save the Planet.

AVAILABLE on AMAZON

Ecallaw walking with his father
shortly before he passed on

About the Author

Ecallaw Leachim has won numerous State and national Titles playing Holdem. He is also a Master Musician, Master Body Worker, Master Numerologist, Dice Master, Recording Artist, Songwriter, and Publisher. On top of all this he is also a prolific writer with over seventeen titles in print.

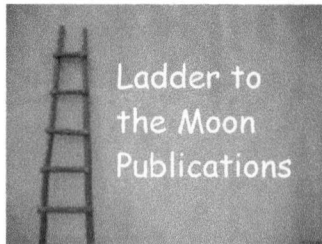

Ladder to
the Moon
Publications

www.laddertothemoon.com.au

Aiming for the Stars is much easier if we stop off at the Moon. We are then out of the atmosphere of our past, and can see things more clearly. We are lighter, can jump higher and further than ever before, and it takes far less energy to start each journey.

The hard part is climbing that Ladder to the Moon.